VISUAL QUICKSTART GUIDE

ACROBAT 3

FOR MACINTOSH AND WINDOWS

TED ALSCH

Pes

Visual QuickStart Guide

ACROBAT 3
FOR MACINTOSH AND WINDOWS

Ted Alspach

Peachpit Press
2414 Sixth Street
Berkeley, CA 94710
(510) 548-4393
(510) 548-5991 (fax)
(800) 283-9444
Find us on the World Wide Web at http://www.peachpit.com
Peachpit Press is a division of Addison Wesley Longman

ISBN: 0-201-68848-4

0 9 8 7 6 5 4 3 2 1

Printed and bound in the United States of America

First Printing March 1997

About the Author

Ted Alspach is the author of several books on desktop publishing and graphics, as well as hundreds of articles on related topics.

Ted is the owner of Bezier Inc., located in the untamed desert somewhere in the middle of Arizona.

Please send any comments regarding this book to Ted at:

AcrobatBookComments@bezier.com

and please visit VectorVille, a site dedicated to vector graphics, at:

http://www.bezier.com/vectorville

Other books by Ted Alspach

Illustrator Studio Secrets

Macworld Illustrator 6 Bible

*Photoshop Complete**

Illustrator Filter Finesse†

The Complete Idiot's Guide to Photoshop

Internet E-mail Quick Tour

KPT Studio Secrets††

The Complete Idiot's Guide to QuarkXPress

Microsoft Bob† (embarrassing, isn't it?)

*The Mac Internet Tour Guide, 2nd Ed.**

The Complete Idiot's Guide to Microsoft Word 6 for the Macintosh

Macworld Illustrator 5.0/5.5 Bible

*With other contributors   †with Jennifer Alspach   ††with Steven Frank

Acknowledgements

Even though this book has my name plastered all over it, it has really been the work of several different people; I couldn't ever do a project like this alone. Some of the most important of those people are:

Nancy Davis, my tireless editor at Peachpit, who molded this book from the lump of clay I sent her into the exquisite porcelain vase you have in front of you.

Scott Calamar at LightSpeed Publishing for keeping my prose in line. Many a "t" would have not been crossed were it not for his incredible attention to detail.

Jennifer Alspach, who as usual went beyond the call of spousal duties to assist with various phases of this book.

Rob Teeple, who did an incredible technical edit for this book, and is the reason you'll never get a "server is not responding message" from bezier.com.

Sandee Cohen, my favorite Visual QuickStart Guide author (for FreeHand and KPT).

Everyone at Peachpit Press who helped move this book along until it hit paper.

And finally, the odd collection of individuals who in some fashion made this book happen: Steve Broback, Steve Roth, and Toby Malina at Thunder Lizard Productions (best conferences you'll ever go to) for thinking of me for Acrobat sessions for the Adobe Internet Conferences; Glenn Fleishman for not ignoring them; Dan Turner at MacAddict for pushing me towards Peachpit, and Jeremy Judson at Peachpit for not pushing me away.

Colophon

This book was created using:

Adobe Photoshop 4.0 (image touch up)

QuarkXPress 3.3 (page layout)

Flash-It! 3.0.2 (screen captures)

Adobe Illustrator 6.0.1 (illustrations)

VectorTools 2.0 (illustrations)

on both

a Power Macintosh 8100/80

and a UMAX S900L/200 Mac clone

Adobe Garamond was used for the body copy, while Futura Extra Black Condensed was used to create the headings.

Book Design: Ted Alspach

Editor: Nancy Davis

Copy Editor: Scott Calamar, LightSpeed Productions

Technical Editor: Robert Teeple

Index: Rebecca Plunkett

TABLE OF CONTENTS

A C R O B A T   R E A D E R   I N   D E P T H

4

U S I N G   P D F   W R I T E R

5

Table of Contents

Table of Contents

Table of Contents

LINKS

9

EDITING PDF FILES
WITH ILLUSTRATOR

10

PLUG-INS

11

FORMS

12

MULTIMEDIA

13

CAPTURE

14

SECURITY

15

Table of Contents

Table of Contents

INTRODUCTION

If you've never used Acrobat before, you're in for quite a pleasant experience when you learn about some of the amazing things it can do. If you've only used Acrobat to read PDF documents given to you, you'll be amazed at what can be done on the "other side;" that is, the creation and editing of Acrobat documents. If you've used Acrobat version 2.1 or older, you'll be astonished by how many new features and capabilities are included in this release. And if you've used Acrobat 3 at all, this book will guide you through it's amazingly deep and complex options, so you can make the most out of your PDF pages.

Acrobat 3 is a quantum leap forward from previous versions of the software. What was once a little set of tools (Acrobat Reader, Acrobat Exchange, Acrobat Distiller) for creating documents that could be viewed on any platform in as good (or better) quality than a paper printout has transformed into a single product that Adobe now just calls "Acrobat," which includes not just the original components, but additional programs and many new capabilities. Even better, Acrobat Reader is free to everyone with a computer running almost any current system software. So it doesn't matter if you have a Macintosh, a Windows 95 system, an OS/2 system, or even a UNIX-based system.

Macintosh and Windows Users

Normally, I'm not a big fan of cross-platform books, as somehow I always end up alienating one platform or the other. In this book, however, I thought it was appropriate to try it; after all, Acrobat is more cross-platform than Java and ASCII.

So, except for a few pages where "Macintosh" or "Windows" is indicated (there are some differences in the print mechanisms of each operating system that are different enough to warrant explanation), each page and example is designed to be used on any platform (currently Macintosh and Windows 95) the Acrobat product family works with.

If you have a UNIX system or a different operating system that Acrobat Reader is created for, the sections on Acrobat Reader will be relevant to you, while the creation and editing sections will not be.

How to use this book

If you've never used a Visual QuickStart Guide from Peachpit Press (of which there are dozens, covering every major software package), then

you'll be pleasantly surprised as well. This book works through the basics of Acrobat Reader through the many intricacies of Acrobat Exchange, in a format that is both easy to understand, and fun to read. Examples are presented so you can follow right along on your computer, comparing what you see on screen to the pictures on each page. All of the typical tasks you would use Acrobat for are included, as well as other, not-so-common ones that you'll find useful when you start to move beyond the basics.

The book is designed that if you were to read it from front to back, you could do so without having to do any flipping or cross referencing.

Most of the examples are presented in the following fashion:

To work through an example:

1. Find the appropriate topic in the Table of Contents, the Index, or by flipping through the pages looking at the thumb tabs.

2. Go to the page where the example appears. (See, this *is* easy).

3. Read that example's steps.

4. At your computer, go through the steps one by one, following the directions on each page.

Most of the pages contain just one example with several illustrations and screenshots. The pages before and after each example contain related example tasks that you might find helpful.

Why I'm a PDF convert

I've been a PDF user ever since Acrobat was first released (version 1.0), but version 3.0 contains the features that I've always wanted. Things like font subset embedding, byteserving capabilities, and compact file sizes (which are almost always much smaller than their original "native" file formats) have made PDF files the standard which no other cross-platform document creator can match.

Visit my web site (www.bezier.com) to view online PDF pages that show some new ways I'm taking advantage of PDF documents.

Finally, Acrobat 3 has allowed me to permanently abandon Macromedia Director 5, the behemoth of multimedia applications I've used for years to create interactive presentations. Look for any future books I write that contain CD-ROMs (this, unfortunately, is not one of them), to have fully interactive multimedia tutorials based entirely on Acrobat 3 technology.

Adobe Acrobat is truly amazing software. It lets anyone with almost any computer system read any document. It doesn't matter if the document was created with Microsoft Word, Adobe PageMaker, QuarkXPress, Adobe Illustrator, or even something as obscure as Jimmy T's Gold DTP Generator (version 3.1). If you can print some or all of the document from the creating program, that document can be quickly saved as an Acrobat file, commonly known as a Portable Document Format, or PDF.

Anyone with the Acrobat Reader software (which is free) can then open and view the document, with the contents looking *exactly* the way they did in the original "authoring" program.

The following pages contain an overview of the Acrobat software, and the Acrobat process. It's a great way to grasp what that Acrobat can do for you.

Introduction to Adobe Acrobat

TM

A brief history of the world (before Acrobat)

Once upon a time, there was a giant computer in a building on the university of a great campus. Okay, truth be told, the building *was* the computer. The computer ran on giant vacuum tubes and did such complex computations as figuring out the square root of 16 (which, it turns out, happened to be 4, according to the computing monstrosity). As the first computer ever, there were few compatibility problems with competing software from rival software publishers. Everything was hunky-dory for about thirty years.

At the end of the 1970s, the personal computer revolution began in earnest when two guys in a garage formed Apple computer. Not long afterwards, other computer manufacturers hopped on the PC (short for Personal Computer back then—you can tell from photos of the 70s that no one cared about being Politically Correct) bandwagon. Suddenly there were all sorts of PCs being made, and there was proprietary software for each computer system.

By the 90s, there were two survivors of the great PC wars, Microsoft and Apple, with various UNIX computer system manufacturers taking up the remaining market share. But a problem remained. How could Joe, who used a PC and Adobe PageMaker, send all his files to his good buddies who used FrameMaker on a UNIX system and QuarkXPress on a Macintosh?

More often than not, Joe would end up printing out his PageMaker documents and his good buddies (who at this time were beginning to distinctly dislike Joe) would have to recreate the document on their machines, with their software. It was all very frustrating and irritating to Joe and his former friends.

Acrobat to the rescue

When Acrobat 1.0 appeared just a few short years ago, Adobe thought they were solving that very problem; Acrobat users could create Acrobat (PDF) files out of any document, and then that document could be ported to any system, regardless of its hardware or software. The only thing they needed in common was the Acrobat software.

An alternate history of the world (mostly before Acrobat)

The World Wide Web has been around since the 70s. Until just a few years ago, however, no one thought about doing all the cool web stuff you now see. In a two-year span that the media erroneously refers to as "overnight," the Web became the center of the computer world, overshadowing king-to-be Multimedia and leaving the grand old ruling party of desktop publishing way back in the dust.

Everyone (all the software publishers, anyway) was pretty much caught off guard by the emergence of the Web, including our good buddies at Adobe.

Then one day some bright young engineer looked at Acrobat, looked at his Web browser, back at Acrobat, and so on, until he had an idea (not to mention an impending appointment with a chiropractor). Why not use Acrobat to distribute content on the Web? The engineer got really busy and a few weeks (so the legend goes) later, Acrobat 3.0 was available. Acrobat 3 includes the ability to create Web pages that aren't that nasty HTML hooey, but instead consist of beautiful-looking pages with custom fonts and illustrations.

How is Acrobat 3 different from its predecessors?

- Acrobat Reader 3 comes as a plug-in for Netscape Navigator and Internet Explorer, allowing Reader users to view PDF files one page at a time right on the Web

- Forms processing has more flexibility than HTML allows

- A Capture plug-in scans documents directly into PDF files

- Seamless links between PDF documents and URLs on the Internet

- Multimedia elements (such as animation) can be added to any PDF file

- Progressive rendering of text and graphics

The components of Acrobat

Acrobat consists of several "parts," each of which is discussed throughout this book.

Acrobat Reader is the software that allows you to view PDF documents. Acrobat Reader is free.

The commercial version of Acrobat contains the following parts:

Acrobat Exchange is the program used to customize PDF files by editing them and adding PDF-specific features like buttons and the ability to be downloaded from the Web one page at a time.

Acrobat Distiller changes PostScript files into PDF files quickly and (for the most part) easily.

Acrobat PDF Writer is the print driver that generates PDF files within any application. Instead of sending your document to a printer, you create a PDF file using the PDF Writer driver.

Acrobat Capture is a plug-in within Acrobat Exchange that lets desktop scanner users scan in documents and convert them to PDFs on the fly. A more robust version is available as a separate product.

What's New in 3.0/Acrobat Components

The Acrobat Reader screen

Shown below, the Acrobat Reader screen is a subset of the Acrobat Exchange screen. The toolbar along the top of the document window provides quick access to most viewing and navigational commands. The Info bar along the bottom provides onscreen information as well as alternative methods for viewing and navigating throughout any PDF document.

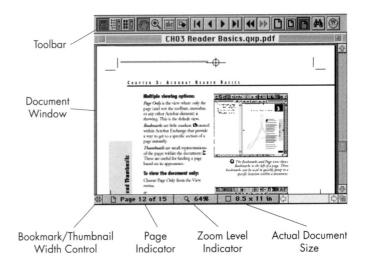

Toolbar

Document Window

Bookmark/Thumbnail Width Control

Page Indicator

Zoom Level Indicator

Actual Document Size

The Acrobat Reader Toolbar

The majority of tools in Acrobat Reader are used for viewing and navigating through PDF documents. Other tools in the toolbar select text and graphics, initiate the Find command, and activate a Web browser.

Page Only   Hand (Scroll)   Select Text

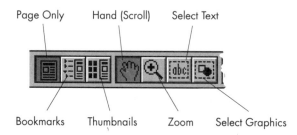

Bookmarks   Thumbnails   Zoom   Select Graphics

First Page   Last Page   Next View

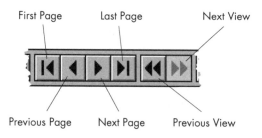

Previous Page   Next Page   Previous View

Actual Size   Find

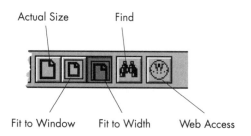

Fit to Window   Fit to Width   Web Access

The Acrobat Reader Toolbar

Acrobat mini glossary

Acrobat	The collection of software used for creating, editing, and viewing PDF files.
Adobe Type Manager	Software that enables PostScript fonts to be displayed at any point size on screen without a noticeable loss of quality. Adobe Type Manager is often referred to as ATM by Macintosh and Windows users.
Bookmarks	Section headings created within Acrobat Exchange that provide quick access to specific portions of a PDF document.
Crop	To remove excess area around the outside edge of a document page.
Distiller	Acrobat Distiller converts PostScript files (including PostScript files printed to disk) into PDF files.
Document	A file containing one or more pages of text and/or graphics
Downsample	To lower the resolution (and the file size) of a bitmap image. For instance, a 300 dpi image will often be downsampled to 72 dpi.
Exchange	Acrobat Exchange is used for viewing and editing PDF files. Exchange has the ability to add form information, buttons, and other PDF-specific elements to a PDF file. Basic text editing can be done within Exchange.
FTP	File Transfer Protocol. The standard protocol for sending and receiving files on the Internet.
Font Embedding	PDF files can include font information within the file, which allows anyone viewing (or printing) the file to view or print the original fonts.
GIF	An image format that includes interlacing and transparency, but is typically limited to 256 colors.
HTML	HyperText Markup Language. The standard for Web pages on the World Wide Web.
JPEG	An image format (JPEG stands for Joint Photographic Experts Group) used to compress images dramatically with a minimum of loss.
Navigation	Moving around within a document.

Mini Glossary

Acrobat mini glossary (continued)

PDF   Portable Document Format. The file format used by Acrobat software. PDF files are exactly the same on Windows, Macintosh, and UNIX platforms.

PDF Writer   Part of the Acrobat software package, PDF Writer allows any application to print directly to a PDF file.

Plug-ins   Additional components added to an application. Acrobat Capture is a plug-in that ships with Acrobat Exchange.

PostScript   A page-description language developed by Adobe Systems, currently the standard language for laser printers and image-setters.

Reader   Acrobat Reader is used to view and print PDF files.

Search   Acrobat Search provides searching capabilities on the text of PDF files.

Thumbnail   A miniature version of a document page, shown to the left of the full-size document in Thumbnail view.

Toolbar   The rack of tools positioned along the top of the document window.

Mini Glossary

7

Acrobat Reader menus

Acrobat Reader Menus

File

Open...	▶
Close	⌘W
Document Info	▶
Page Setup...	⌘⇧P
Print...	⌘P
Preferences	▶
Quit	⌘Q

The File menu contains commands used for document management.

Edit

Undo	⌘Z
Cut	⌘H
Copy	⌘C
Paste	⌘U
Clear	
Select All	⌘A
Properties...	⌘I

The Edit menu contains commands used for retrieving and selecting text and objects within PDF documents.

View

Actual Size	⌘H
Fit Page	⌘J
Fit Width	⌘K
Fit Visible	⌘M
Zoom To...	⌘L
Full Screen	⌘⇧L
First Page	⌘1
Previous Page	⌘2
Next Page	⌘3
Last Page	⌘4
Go To Page...	⌘5
Go Back	⌘-
Go Forward	⌘=
✓ Single Page	
Continuous	
Continuous - Facing Pages	
Articles...	⌘⇧A
✓ Page Only	⌘6
Bookmarks and Page	⌘7
Thumbnails and Page	⌘8

The View menu contains commands used for viewing and navigating through PDF documents.

Tools

🖐 Hand	⌘⌥1
🔍 Zoom In	⌘⌥2
✓ 🔤 Select Text	⌘⌥4
🔲 Select Graphics	⌘⌥5
Find...	⌘F
Find Again	⌘G
Find Next Note	⌘T

The Tools menu contains commands used for selecting tools and searching for text and notes within PDF documents.

Window

Hide Toolbar	⌘⇧B
Visit Adobe's Web Site	
Hide Menubar	⌘⇧M
Show Clipboard	
Cascade	
Tile Horizontally	
Tile Vertically	
Close All	⌘⌥W
✓ CH03 Reader Basics.qxp.pdf	

The Window menu contains commands used for displaying and hiding Reader components and PDF document windows.

PDF files are created by Acrobat software, but most PDF files start out as a different type of document. Some start as ASCII text files. Other, more ambitious documents start as QuarkXPress files and may contain embedded Photoshop and Illustrator files.

This chapter shows you how to use PDF Writer and Acrobat Distiller to create PDF files from the most popular software programs on both Macintosh and Windows platforms.

Where PDF Files Come From

TM

To use the PDF Writer printer driver to create PDF files on a Macintosh:

1. Select Chooser from the Apple menu.

2. In the Chooser, click on the PDF Writer icon. **Ⓐ**

3. Click in the upper-left close box to close the Chooser window. Before it closes, you'll see a dialog box reminding you to check Page Setup in your applications before you print; click the OK button to leave this dialog box.

4. In your application, choose Page Setup from the File menu. Verify that the information there is correct. Click the OK button to verify your changes and close the Page Setup dialog box. **Ⓑ**

5. Select Print from the File menu. The dialog box that appears will be different than the standard printer dialog box you're used to. Enter any appropriate information (page range, etc.) and click the OK button.

6. After you click the OK button, a standard file save dialog box will appear. Enter a name for your PDF file and the location where you'd like to save it.

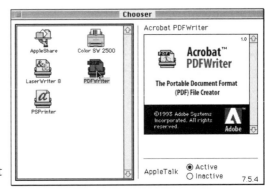

Ⓐ *Select the PDF Writer icon in the Chooser.*

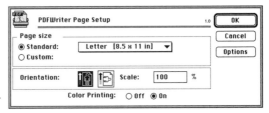

Ⓑ *Verify all the information is correct in Page Setup.*

> The PDF Writer icon that appears in the Chooser is an actual file that exists in your Extensions folder. Don't accidentally move or delete this file!
>
> **MACINTOSH TIP**

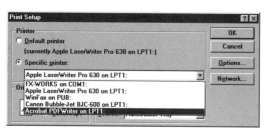

Select the Acrobat PDF Writer from the printer list.

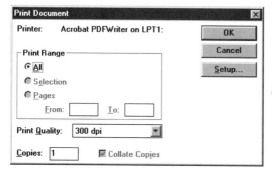

D *Click OK in the the Print Document dialog box to create a PDF File.*

To use the PDF Writer printer driver to create PDF files with Windows:

1. Within an application, choose Print Setup from the File menu.

2. In the Print Setup dialog box, select Acrobat PDFWriter from the printer drop-down list. **C**

3. Click in the upper-right close box to close the Print Setup window.

4. Select Print from the File menu. The dialog box that appears will be different than the standard printer dialog box you're used to. Enter any appropriate information (page range, etc.) and click the OK button. **D**

5. After you click the OK button, a standard file save dialog box will appear. Enter a name for your PDF file and the location where you'd like to save it.

6. After you name the file, you'll be presented with a window for entering PDF Writer information. Entering information is optional. Click OK when you've finished.

Using PDF Writer with Windows

To create a PostScript file on a Macintosh:

1. Within any application, choose Print from the File menu.

2. Select the File option in the Destination area of the Print dialog box and click the OK button. **Ⓔ**

3. Name the PostScript file and select a location for it.

Ⓔ *Select the File Radio Button in the Print dialog box.*

To create a PostScript file with Windows:

1. Within any application, choose Print from the File menu. The Print Document dialog box appears.

2. Click the Setup button in the Print Document dialog box.

3. Click the Options button in the Print Setup dialog box. The Properties window for that printer will be displayed.

4. Click the PostScript tab. **Ⓕ**

5. Choose the Encapsulated PostScript (EPS) option. Click OK.

6. Click OK to exit the Print Setup dialog box. Click OK in the Print Document dialog box, and the PostScript file will be created.

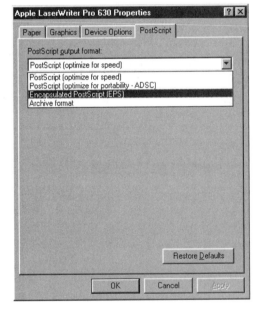

Ⓕ *Select the EPS option in the PostScript tab of the Printer Properties dialog box.*

Creating PostScript Files

PDF files can be created from existing PostScript files (see preceding page on how to create PostScript files).

To create a PDF file with Acrobat Distiller (Mac and Windows):

1. Select the PostScript file that you want to convert into a PDF file.

2. Drag the PostScript file on top of the Acrobat Distiller icon.

3. Acrobat Distiller will automatically "distill" the PostScript file into a PDF file, adding the ".PDF" tag to the end of the file name. For example, a PostScript file called "QuickStart.ps" would be saved by Distiller as "QuickStart.ps.pdf."

Distiller options are discussed in detail in Chapter 6: Using Acrobat Distiller.

Creating PDF Files with Acrobat Distiller

Acrobat Reader is software that allows anyone to read PDF (Portable Document Format) files. There's a Reader for Macintosh, Windows, and Unix platforms, and all PDF files are completely cross-platform. No matter which system the original PDF file was created on, it can be read on any other system. This is just one of the strengths of Acrobat Reader.

To make sure everyone can get Acrobat Reader to read any PDF files, Adobe provides the software free on the official Adobe Web site (www.adobe.com). The software is easy to install (see the next two pages for installation instructions for Macintosh and Windows systems), and it only takes up a few megabytes of hard disk space. Acrobat Reader needs about 4MB of RAM to run.

An additional component of the Reader software allows it to be used within the popular Web browsers like Netscape Navigator, enabling it to read one page at a time from Web sites all over the world.

TM

To install Acrobat Reader on your Macintosh:

1. Find the Acrobat Reader Installer icon and double-click on it. **Ⓐ** This will launch the installation software.

2. Click the Continue button when the main screen appears. **Ⓑ**

3. Select the folder and disk in which you want to install the software, and then press the Install button. If you don't specify a location, the default location will be the top level of your startup drive. The installer automatically quits any applications that had been running.

As Acrobat Reader installs itself, a progress bar fills in from left to right. You can stop the installation at any time by clicking the Stop button.

4. After installation, click the Restart button. Your computer will restart, loading any new system extensions required for Acrobat reader.

5. Verify Acrobat Reader has been installed properly by opening the folder where it was installed. **Ⓒ**

Ⓐ *Double-click the Reader installer.*

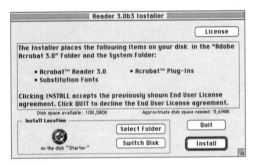

Ⓑ *Select the disk and folder before clicking the Install button.*

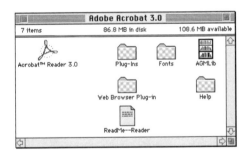

Ⓒ *After restarting your Macintosh, the Acrobat Reader application will be fully installed and ready to use.*

Installing Acrobat Reader for Macintosh

> For best results, restart your Macintosh with extensions off (press the Shift key during startup) when installing new software.
>
> **MACINTOSH TIP**

O *Double-click on the Reader Installer icon.*

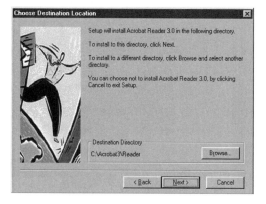

O *Choose the Directory path before clicking the Next button.*

O *The Acrobat Reader Application window shown after installation.*

To install Acrobat Reader on your Windows system:

1. Find the Acrobat Reader Installer file (usually called w32rd) and double-click on it. **O** This will launch the installation software.

2. Click the Next button when the Welcome screen appears.

3. Click the Yes button on the Software License Agreement screen.

4. The installer will select a location on your hard drive automatically, and display the directory path in the Destination Directory window. **O**

To change the directory, click the browse button. If the directory is correct, click the Next button.

As Acrobat Reader installs itself, a progress bar fills in from left to right. You can stop the installation at any time by clicking the Cancel button.

5. After installation, click the Finish button. Click OK in the dialog box that follows. The Installer will then quit.

6. Verify Acrobat Reader has been installed properly by opening the directory where it was installed. **O**

Installing Acrobat Reader for Windows

To run Acrobat Reader:

Double-click on the Acrobat Reader icon (located in the Acrobat folder). **G**

To open an existing PDF file in Acrobat Reader:

1. Choose Open from the File menu. **H**

2. Select the file you wish to open and click the Open button. **I**

or

Double-click on the PDF file icon. **J**

or

Drag the PDF file icon on top of the Acrobat Reader icon. **K**

G Double-click on the Acrobat Reader icon to run the application.

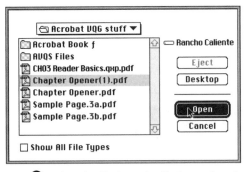

H Choose Open from the File menu.

K Drag a PDF file on top of the Acrobat Reader icon.

To close an open PDF file:

Choose Close Window from the File menu.

or

(Macintosh) Click the close box in the upper-left corner of the document window.

or

(Windows) Click the close (X) box in the upper-right corner of the docu-

I Select the file from the file list within the Open dialog box.

J Double-click on a PDF file to open it in Acrobat Reader.

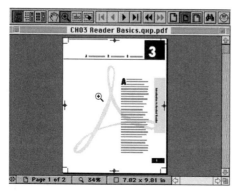

O *The Zoom tool is accessible from the toolbar positioned under the menu bar.*

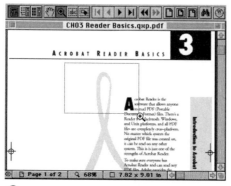

M *Click on the area of a document you wish to zoom in on.*

To zoom in on a PDF document:

1. Select the Zoom tool on the Acrobat toolbar. **O**

2. Click on the area you wish to zoom in on. **M** Releasing the mouse button will magnify that area.

To zoom in on a specific area of a PDF Document:

1. Select the Zoom tool on the Acrobat toolbar.

2. Drag a marquee (a rectangular dashed line) with the Zoom tool around the particular area you want to zoom in on. **N**
That area will fill the screen when you release the mouse button.

N *To zoom in on a specific area, drag around that area with the zoom tool.*

Each click of the Zoom tool doubles the current magnification (from 100% to 200% to 400% and so on).

ACROBAT 3 TIP

Zooming In

To zoom out of a PDF document:

1. Select the Zoom tool from the toolbar. **O**

2. Press the Option key (Mac) or Alt key (Windows). The middle of the magnifying glass will display a minus (–) sign. **P**

3. Click while keeping the Option or Alt key pressed. **Q** The page will zoom out to one-half the previous magnification (i.e., 100% will become 50%, 50% will become 25%). **R**

O *The Zoom tool is accessible from the toolbar positioned under the menu bar.*

P *The Magnifying Glass (Zoom tool) will display a minus sign when the Option key (Mac) or Alt key (Windows) is pressed.*

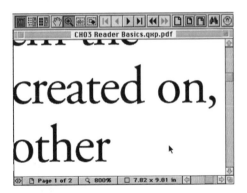

Q *Click on the document with the Zoom Out tool.*

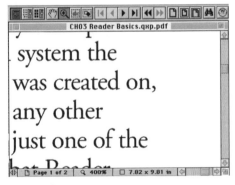

R *The page is reduced to one-half the previous zoom setting.*

Zooming Out

> To access the Zoom tool using the keyboard, press Command-Option-2.
>
> **MACINTOSH TIP**

> To access the Zoom tool using the keyboard, press Ctrl+Shift+2.
>
> **WINDOWS TIP**

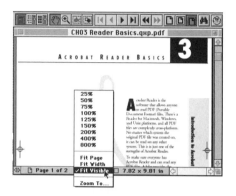

S *The zoom level pop-up menu is found in the lower left of each document window.*

T *Once you select a zoom level from the zoom level pop-up menu, the document will zoom to that size.*

View	Tools	Window
Actual Size		⌘H
Fit Page		⌘J
Fit Width		⌘K
Fit Visible		⌘M
Zoom To...		⌘L
Full Screen		⌘⇧L
First Page		⌘1
Previous Page		⌘2
Next Page		⌘3
Last Page		⌘4
Go To Page...		⌘5
Go Back		⌘-
Go Forward		⌘=
✓Single Page		
Continuous		
Continuous - Facing Pages		
Articles...		⌘⇧A
✓Page Only		⌘6
Bookmarks and Page		⌘7
Thumbnails and Page		⌘8

U *The View menu provides another method for selecting preset zooms.*

In addition to using the Zoom tool to change the magnification of your document, there are several different preset zoom levels that are easily accessible from within Acrobat Reader.

To use the preset zoom levels:

1. Press and hold on the zoom level indicator along the lower left of the document window. **S**

2. Select a preset zoom from the menu that appears.

The document will be displayed at the size you select. **T**

or

Select a preset zoom level from the available options under the View menu. **U** The View menu only shows the named views (Actual Size, Fit Page, Fit Width, Fit Visible).

The Preset Zoom Levels

Fit Page, Fit Width, and Fit Visible are arbitrary zoom levels with no particular zoom percentage assigned to them. The resulting zoom percentage is based on the window size of the current document.

ACROBAT 3 TIP

If you'd like your document to appear at a specific zoom level percentage that isn't one of the preset zoom levels, follow the steps below.

To display a document at a specific zoom level:

1. Click (do not press and hold) on the zoom level indicator along the lower left of the document window. **V** The Zoom To dialog box will appear.

or

Select Zoom To from the View menu. **W**
The Zoom To dialog box will appear. **X**

2. Type the magnification you desire and click the OK button or press the Enter key. The document will be displayed at the magnification you specified.

V *Click once on the zoom level indicator.*

W *Select Zoom To from the View menu.*

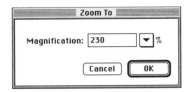

X *Enter your desired magnification in the Zoom To dialog box and click the OK button or press the Enter key.*

Zooming to a Specific Zoom Percentage

View

Actual Size	⌘H
✓Fit Page	⌘J
Fit Width	⌘K
Fit Visible	⌘M
Zoom To...	⌘L
Full Screen	⌘⇧L
First Page	⌘1
Previous Page	⌘2
Next Page	⌘3
Last Page	⌘4
Go To Page...	⌘5
Go Back	⌘-
Go Forward	⌘=
✓Single Page	
Continuous	
Continuous – Facing Pages	
Articles...	⌘⇧A
✓Page Only	⌘6
Bookmarks and Page	⌘7
Thumbnails and Page	⌘8

❻ *Choose Full Screen from the View menu to hide everything but the document.*

❼ *Full Screen mode hides everything that isn't part of your PDF document.*

To hide everything but the document:

Choose Full Screen from the View menu. **❻** Everything but the current document will be hidden, including the menu bar and other application windows. **❼**

To "unhide" everything that was hidden:

Press the ESC key on your keyboard. The document will display at the previous view (as it was displayed prior to viewing the document in Full Screen mode).

> **MACINTOSH TIP**
> To quickly enter Full Screen mode, press Command-L

> **WINDOWS TIP**
> To quickly enter Full Screen mode, press Control+Shift+L

> **ACROBAT 3 TIP**
> Working in Full Screen mode requires that you know many of the key commands for navigating and zooming within Acrobat Reader.

Hiding Everything but the Document

Moving Around within a Page

Many Acrobat pages are too large to fit on your monitor at a size to be read without incurring permanent squint damage. Unfortunately, this means part of the page is cropped by the edge of your monitor, or more accurately, by the edge of your document window. And, since everyone knows that scroll bars are way too inconvenient to use all the time, Acrobat Reader provides several other methods for navigating within a single document page.

To move around freely within a page:

1. Select the Hand tool from the toolbar along the top of the page. **AA**

2. Click on the page and drag (keep the mouse button pressed as you move the mouse) to reposition the page. **BB**

3. Release the mouse button and the page will stay at the new position. **CC**

To move down within a page:

Press the Page Down key on your keyboard.

To move up within a page:

Press the Page Up key on your keyboard.

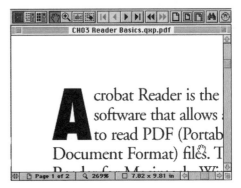

AA *Select the Hand tool to move the document within the document window.*

Click and drag to reposition a document within the window. **BB**

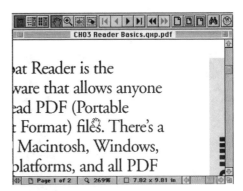

CC *Release the mouse button and the page will stay in the new position.*

Press the Page Down key when the bottom of a page is showing to move to the top of the next page in the document. Likewise, press the Page Up key when the top of a page is showing to move to the previous page.

ACROBAT 3 TIP

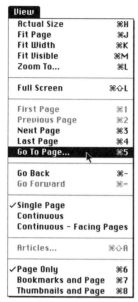

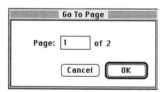

To go to any page within a document, choose *Go To Page* from the View menu.

Enter a page number and click the OK button to go to that page.

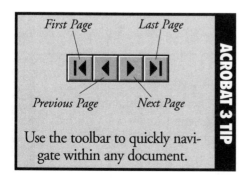

First Page   Last Page

Previous Page   Next Page

ACROBAT 3 TIP

Use the toolbar to quickly navigate within any document.

To view the next page in a document:

Press the Down Arrow key.

or

Choose Next Page from the View menu.

To view the previous page in a document:

Press the Up Arrow key.

or

Choose Previous Page from the View menu.

To go to a specific page in a document:

1. Choose Go To Page from the View menu.

2. Enter the page that you'd like to go to and click the OK button or press Enter.

To go to the first page in a document:

Choose First Page from the View menu.

or

Press the Home key.

To go to the last page in a document:

Choose Last Page from the View menu.

or

Press the End key.

Document Navigation

Multiple viewing options:

Page Only is the view where only the page (and not the toolbars, menu bar, or any other Acrobat element) is showing. This is the default view.

Bookmarks are little markers created within Acrobat Exchange that provide a way to get to a specific section of a page instantly.

Thumbnails are small representations of the pages within the document. These are useful for finding a page based on its appearance.

To view the document only:

Choose Page Only from the View menu.

or

Click on the Page Only button on the toolbar.

To view a document with Bookmarks:

Choose Bookmarks and Page from the View menu. **FF**

or

Click on the Bookmark button on the toolbar.

To view a document with Thumbnails:

Choose Thumbnails and Page from the View menu. **GG**

or

Click on the Thumbnail button.

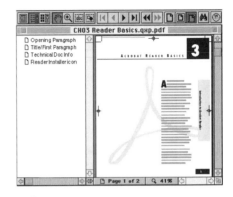

FF *The Bookmarks and Page view shows Bookmarks to the left of a page. These bookmarks can be used to quickly jump to a specific location within a document.*

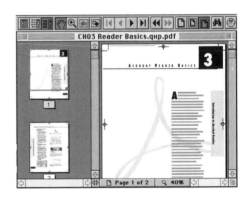

GG *The Thumbnails and Page view shows little thumbnails of each page to the left of the document. Clicking on a thumbnail takes you directly to that page.*

Bookmark and Thumbnail views reduce the page size substantially on screen, often making text difficult to read.

ACROBAT 3 TIP

Viewing Bookmarks and Thumbnails

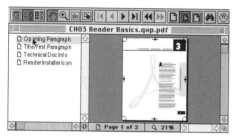

(HH) *Click on the Bookmark button.*

(II) *Click on the appropriate bookmark.*

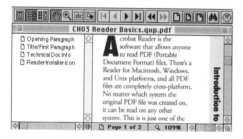

(JJ) *The Bookmark location is displayed instantly.*

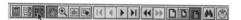

(KK) *Click on the Thumbnail button.*

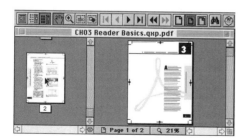

(LL) *Click on the appropriate thumbnail.*

To use Bookmarks to go to a specific spot within a document:

1. Click the Bookmark button on the toolbar. **(HH)**

2. Click on the Bookmark that describes the spot you want to view. **(II)** The page and location of that Bookmark will appear on the screen. **(JJ)**

To use Thumbnails to go to a specific page within a document:

1. Click the Thumbnail button on the toolbar. **(KK)**

2. Click on the Thumbnail that represents the page you want to view. **(LL)** That page will appear on the screen.

> Bookmarks contain location information (page and position) and zoom level information. They are often used to highlight a small portion of a document, forcing that small portion to fill up the entire viewing area.
>
> **ACROBAT 3 TIP**

Using Bookmarks and Thumbnails

Printing a PDF Document (Macintosh)

To print a PDF document from Acrobat Reader (Macintosh):

1. Choose Print from the File menu (or Press Command–P).

2. Enter the number of copies in the Print dialog box. 🔵

3. Enter the page range (starting and ending page numbers) in the From: and To: text fields.

4. Click the Print button to send the document to the printer. Clicking Cancel will return you to your document without printing anything.

🔵 *Choose Print from the File menu.*

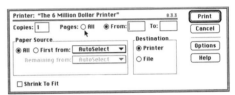

🔵 *In the Print dialog box, enter the number of copies and the Page range. Then click the Print button.*

> **MACINTOSH TIP**
>
> Acrobat Reader (or the full Acrobat product) must have been installed via the Installer in order to print documents correctly.

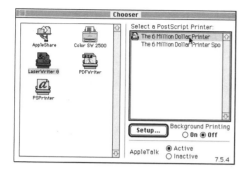

⓪ *The Chooser window allows you to select a printer.*

To choose a printer (Macintosh):

1. Select Chooser from the Apple menu (at the far left of the menu bar).

2. Click on the LaserWriter icon in the Chooser Window. **⓪** If printing to another type of printer, click on the appropriate printer type.

3. Select the printer from the list of printers (hey, even if you only have one printer, it's still a list).

4. Close the Chooser window. The next time the Print dialog box opens, the new printer will be selected.

Choosing a Printer (Macintosh)

To print a PDF document from Acrobat Reader (Windows):

1. Choose Print from the File menu (or press Control+P).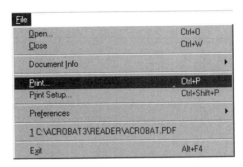

2. Enter the number of copies in the Print dialog box. **QQ**

3. Enter the page range (starting and ending page numbers) in the From: and To: text fields.

4. Click the OK button to send the document to the printer. Clicking Cancel will return you to your document without printing anything.

PP *Choose Print from the File menu.*

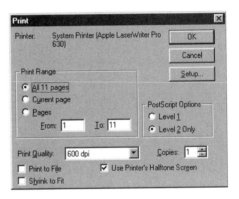

QQ *In the Print dialog box, enter the number of copies and the page range and then click the OK button.*

To select a printer (Windows):

1. Choose Print Setup from the File menu (or press Control+Shift+P).

The Print Setup dialog box will appear. **RR**

2. Select the printer from the Name drop down menu.

3. Change any other options as needed.

4. Click the OK button. The new printer will receive future printouts.

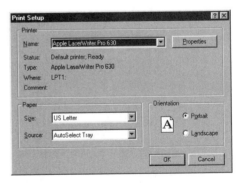

RR *In the Print setup dialog box, select the printer you wish to print to.*

Now that you've mastered the basics of Acrobat Reader, it's time to move on to some of the deep features of Reader that make it such wonderful software for viewing documents.

Often you'll want to go beyond simple document navigation and viewing, to do things such as searching your document for text, copying text or an image from Acrobat Reader, or even changing the many preferences that Reader provides.

This chapter takes you on a tour of Acrobat Reader's nitty gritty details, so you can make the software work for you!

Advanced Acrobat Reader Introduction

™

Reading Document Info

Each PDF document has certain information associated with it. This information may tell you when the document was created, what application created it, or when it was last modified.

To read the Document Info for the current document:

1. Select General from the Document Info submenu in the File menu. You can also press Command-D (Macintosh) or Control+D (Windows). **A**

The General Info dialog box will appear, showing various information. **B** Note that there are four uneditable text boxes in this dialog box. These boxes are editable only within Acrobat Exchange.

The "Optimized" (in this case set to No) label refers to the capability of Acrobat 3 to compress PDF files, allowing them to be read one page at a time via Web browsers and the Acrobat Reader Plug-in.

2. To close the General Info dialog box, click the OK button.

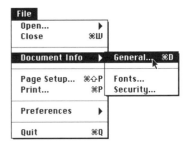

A *Select General from the Document Info submenu.*

B *The General Info window displays information about the current active document.*

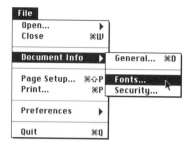

C *Select Fonts from the Document Info submenu.*

To determine which fonts are used in a PDF document:

1. Select Fonts from the Document Info submenu in the File menu. **C**

A list of all the "base" fonts used in the document will appear in the Font Info window. **D**

2. Click the List All Fonts button to see an expanded list of fonts that includes basic styles (bold and italic) applied to fonts within the document. **E**

This listing more accurately depicts the fonts that are used within the PDF file.

3. Click the OK button to close the Font Info window.

D *The Font Info window displays the base fonts used in the PDF document.*

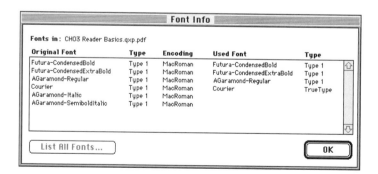

E *Clicking the List All Fonts button shows all variations of fonts used in the PDF file.*

Checking for Font Usage

Acrobat Reader Security

Various levels of security can be applied to any PDF document. These options can prevent someone viewing a PDF document from changing the document (in Exchange), printing the document, opening the document, selecting text and graphics, and adding or changing notes and form fields.

Many of these activities can't be done in Reader because it doesn't have the capability to do such things as changing the document and adding or changing notes and form fields. Those items will always read "Not Allowed" when viewed in Reader, but may show up as "Allowed" in Exchange (which has the tools for doing both of those activities).

To look at the Security options:

1. Select Security from the Document Info submenu in the File menu. **❶**

The Security Info dialog box will appear, displaying all the current security information. **❷**

2. To close the Security Info dialog box, click the OK button.

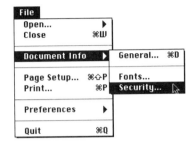

❶ *Select Security from the Document Info submenu.*

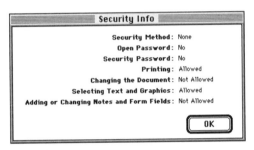

❷ *The Security Info dialog box displays the security options for the current active document.*

34

Tools
✓ 🖐 Hand ⌘⌥1
🔍 Zoom In ⌘⌥2
🔍 Zoom Out ⌘⌥3
[abc] Select Text ⌘⌥4
🔲 Select Graphics ⌘⌥5

Find... ⌘F
Find Again ⌘G

Find Next Note ⌘T

H *Choose Select Text from the Tools menu.*

I *Drag across the text that you want to select, with the Select Text tool.*

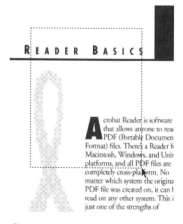

J *With the Select Graphics tool, drag across the area of the page you want to select.*

To select text:

1. Choose the Select Text tool on your toolbar, or choose the Select Text tool from the Tools menu. **H**

2. Drag the Select Text tool over the text that you would like to select. **I**

The Select Text tool selects entire words at once. There is no way to select just a portion of a word.

See the next page for details on how to copy and paste the text you've selected.

Selecting text is pretty straightforward, but selecting graphics is not. In fact, you never actually select graphics. Instead, Acrobat provides a Select Graphics tool that really lets you take a screenshot of a portion of your Reader document (which may include graphics). For graphics which normally print well and display poorly, this tool is practically useless.

To select portions of a displayed PDF document:

1. Choose the Select Graphics tool from the Tools menu.

2. Drag the Select Graphics tool over the area that you would like to select. **J**

The pixels within the selection border represent the area that is selected.

See the next section for details on how to copy and paste the pixels you've selected.

How to Select Text and Graphics

How to cut, copy, and paste selected text or graphics within Acrobat Reader:

Okay, the truth is, you *can't* cut text or graphics in Acrobat Reader. And you can't paste, either. But you can copy, and you can paste what you've copied into another application. So this should really be:

K *Select Copy from the Edit menu.*

How to copy selected text or graphics within Acrobat Reader:

With either text or graphics selected, choose Copy from the Edit menu. **K**

The text or graphics will be copied and be available for pasting in another application.

How to paste copied text or graphics in other applications:

In any program (other than Acrobat Reader), choose Paste from the Edit menu. **L**

The copied text or graphics will appear in the active document of the application.

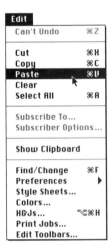

L *In another application, select Paste from the Edit menu.*

Cut, Copy, and Paste

Usually, the default magnification at which PDF files are displayed is preset to a view that may not be the best for your monitor. Fortunately, you can change this setting within Acrobat Reader's preferences.

To change the default magnification:

1. Choose General from the Preferences submenu in the File menu. The General Preferences dialog box appears.

2. Select a new default magnification from the Default Magnification pop-up menu, or type in a new percentage in the text field.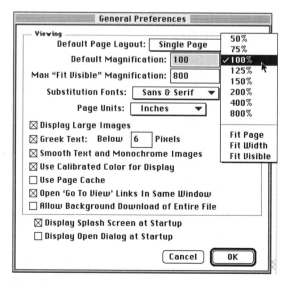

3. Click the OK button (or press Return or Enter).

The new default magnification is now in place. All documents opened in Reader from this point on will be displayed at the new default magnification.

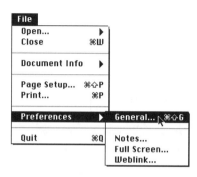

Select General from the Preferences submenu in the File menu.

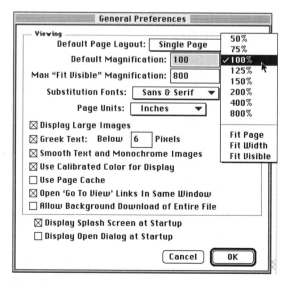

Select a new default magnification from the pop-up menu.

> Many Acrobat Reader users prefer to have one of the "Fit" settings as their default. The Fit Visible option is great for focusing on the content within a page instead of seeing all the white space around that content.
>
> **ACROBAT 3 TIP**

Changing the Default Magnification

If you've ever seen Acrobat zoom in too far when you've changed pages in Fit Visible mode to the point where just one word fills your 37" monitor, you'll appreciate Acrobat Reader's ability to restrict Fit Visible's maximum zoom amount. This prevents pages with just a page number on them from scaring you to death with giant numbers.

To modify maximum resolution in the Fit Visible setting:

1. Choose General from the Preferences submenu in the File menu. **O**

2. Select a new zoom percentage from the pop-up menu next to Max "Fit Visible" Magnification, or type in a new value in the text field. **P**

3. Click the OK button. Now, the Fit Visible magnification setting will never exceed the maximum zoom percentage you've entered.

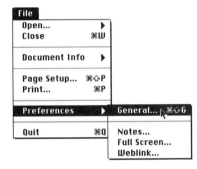

O *Select General from the Preferences Submenu in the File menu.*

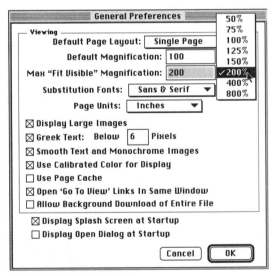

P *Select a new default magnification from the pop-up menu.*

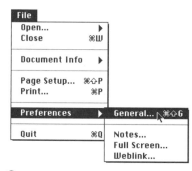

Q *Select General from the Preferences Submenu in the File menu.*

There are a multitude of preferences that can be changed in Acrobat Reader to affect the way you view and navigate through documents. Most of these can be modified through the General Preferences dialog box.

Keep in mind that changes made in Acrobat Reader affect the way you'll view and work with all future documents within Reader only. These changes aren't tied to specific documents, they only affect the way Reader displays documents. To change document preferences you *must* edit the document in Acrobat Exchange.

To change other Reader preferences:

1. Choose General from the Preferences submenu in the File menu. **Q**

2. Make any changes in the General Preferences dialog box. **R**

3. Click the OK button. All changes you've made affect the current and future documents opened in Reader. If you don't like your changes, just re-enter the General Preferences dialog box and undo your changes.

General Preferences

Viewing
Default Page Layout: Single Page
Default Magnification: 100 %
Max "Fit Visible" Magnification: 800 %
Substitution Fonts: Sans & Serif
Page Units: Inches
☒ Display Large Images
☒ Greek Text: Below 6 Pixels
☒ Smooth Text and Monochrome Images
☒ Use Calibrated Color for Display
☐ Use Page Cache
☒ Open 'Go To View' Links In Same Window
☐ Allow Background Download of Entire File

☒ Display Splash Screen at Startup
☐ Display Open Dialog at Startup

Cancel   OK

R *Make any changes in the General Preferences dialog box and then click the OK button.*

If another person uses Acrobat Reader on the machine where you've made your changes, keep in mind that he or she will be stuck with your preferences changes.

ACROBAT 3 TIP

Acrobat Reader 3 has a special "Presentation" mode called Full Screen mode. In this mode, Acrobat Reader documents can display like a slide show, or similar to the way that presentation software like Adobe Persuasion displays screens.

To change to Full Screen mode:

Select Full Screen from the View Menu. ❺

The screen will redraw, zooming the current page to the full size of the screen, hiding the menu bar and toolbar.

To leave Full Screen mode:

Press the ESC key (in the upper left of the keyboard).

The screen will redraw, displaying the menu bar and toolbar, and zooming the current page back to the view that was used prior to the Full Screen mode. ❻

View	
Actual Size	⌘H
✓Fit Page	⌘J
Fit Width	⌘K
Fit Visible	⌘M
Zoom To...	⌘L
Full Screen	⌘⇧L
First Page	⌘1
Previous Page	⌘2
Next Page	⌘3
Last Page	⌘4
Go To Page...	⌘5
Go Back	⌘-
Go Forward	⌘=
✓Single Page	⌘⇧N
Continuous	⌘⇧C
Continuous – Facing Pages	
Articles...	⌘⇧A
✓Page Only	⌘6
Bookmarks and Page	⌘7
Thumbnails and Page	⌘8

❺ *Select Full Screen from the View menu.*

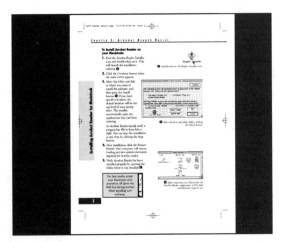

❻ *The Full Screen mode hides the menu bar and toolbar, and zooms the page to fill the screen.*

Without a menu bar or toolbar displayed on screen, Acrobat Reader becomes slightly more difficult to use. If you're like most people, you don't have an extra 2Mb of storage space in your brain to memorize all the Acrobat key commands. Fortunately, there are several preferences for Full Screen mode that can make navigating much easier than it would be otherwise.

To change the Full Screen Preferences:

1. Select Full Screen from the Preferences submenu in the File menu. **U**

2. In the Full Screen Preferences dialog box, make any changes that you believe will make it easier to work in Full Screen mode.

3. Click OK when you're finished making changes to save those changes. **V**

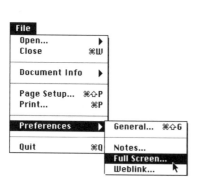

U *Select Full Screen from the Preferences submenu.*

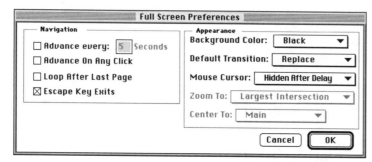

V *Make any desired changes in the Full Screen Preferences dialog box and click OK.*

How to Change the Full Screen Preferences

When a PDF file is edited in Acrobat Exchange, annotations can be added to the document in any area. These notes resemble a tiny document icon when viewed in Acrobat Reader; the text of the note is hidden by default within the little icon. **ⓦ**

To read Acrobat Reader notes:

1. Locate the note that you wish to read on a PDF document.

2. Double-click on the note with the cursor. **ⓧ**

The note will expand to display all its text.

To close expanded Acrobat Reader notes:

Click the close box (in the upper left corner) of the note.

The note will collapse back to the little document icon.

ⓦ *Notes appear as little document icons on a PDF document page.*

In Acrobat Reader, you may click on a note once and drag it around a page, but you may not delete or remove that note. In addition, because you can't save changes to a PDF document in Reader, the note will reappear in its original position the next time you open that document in Reader.

ⓧ *Double-clicking on the note icon displays its contents. Clicking the close box on the expanded note collapses it back to an icon.*

How to Read Embedded Notes

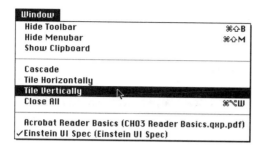

⑦ *Select a Tile option from the Window menu.*

Your computer monitor can get quite messy if you have several Acrobat PDF document windows open at one time in Reader. Fortunately, there are some built-in functions that "clean up" your document windows automatically.

To quickly display all open documents:

Choose either Tile Horizontally or Tile Vertically from the Window menu. ⑦

Tile Horizontally will place open windows in a vertical stack. ⓩ

Tile Vertically will place open windows in a horizontal stack. ⒜⒜

To bring the active window to the front while displaying the title bar of other open documents:

Choose Cascade from the Window menu.

The active (selected) document will appear in the front, while behind it the title bars of all the other documents will be displayed. ⒝⒝

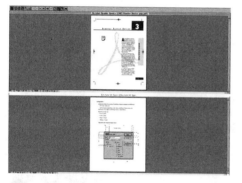

ⓩ *Tile Horizontally displays documents one above another.*

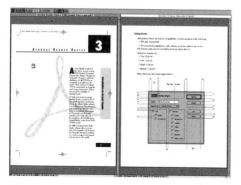

⒜⒜ *Tile Vertically displays documents next to each other.*

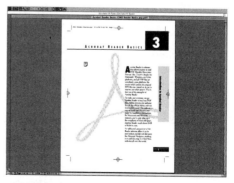

⒝⒝ *Cascade displays the active document in front of the other open documents.*

How to Arrange Multiple Windows

To close all open documents at once without quitting:

Select Close All from the Window menu.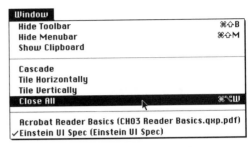

Because Acrobat Reader can't save changes to documents, you'll never be presented with a "Do You Wish To Save Changes" dialog box. Instead, the documents will quickly zip away.

or

Option-click for Macintosh or Alt-click for Windows on the close box of any open documents. This closes all open documents instantly.

To close all open documents at once when quitting Acrobat Reader:

Select Quit from the File menu.

Any open documents are automatically closed when the program is quit. **⑪**

Choosing Close All from the Window menu closes all open documents without quitting Acrobat.

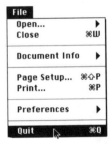

⑪ Choosing Quit from the File menu automatically quits Reader and closes any open documents.

How To Close All Open Documents

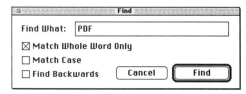

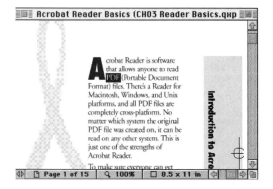

Sometimes it is necessary to locate a particular phrase or word within a document. Instead of searching through the document by reading every page, you can use Acrobat Reader's Find command to do the work for you.

To find a word in a PDF document:

1. Select Find from the Tools menu. ⓔ

The Find palette will appear.

2. Type the word (or words) in the text field that you're looking for. ⓕ

If the word stands alone (like PDF) then check the Match Whole Word Only checkbox.

3. Click the Find button. The first occurrence of that word in the document will be highlighted. ⓖⓖ

To find the next occurrence of a found word in a PDF document:

Select Find Again from the Tools menu. ⓗⓗ

The next occurrence of that word will be highlighted. ⓘ

ⓔ *Choose Find from the Tools menu.*

ⓕ *Enter the word you wish to find and click the Find button.*

ⓖⓖ *The first occurrence of that word will be highlighted.*

ⓗⓗ *Select Find Again to find the next occurrence of a found word.*

ⓘ *The next occurrence of that word will be highlighted.*

How to Find Text

Adobe allows Acrobat Reader to be distributed along with PDF files, as long as all the documentation and original files are included and are not modified in any way. The original installer (Mac or Windows) must be used as the method for distributing Acrobat Reader.

To distribute Acrobat Reader on CD-ROM:

Copy the Acrobat Reader Installer to the CD-ROM master. All of the original Acrobat Reader Installer files must be present.

To distribute Acrobat Reader on the Web:

The best way to do this is to have a link to Adobe's Web site (www.adobe.com) or directly to the Acrobat Reader FTP site (this changes occasionally; check the current address by going to www.adobe.com first). This works better than keeping a copy on your own Web server because Adobe's will always be current.

How to Give Away Acrobat Reader

There are several ways to create PDF documents, but by far the simplest is by using Acrobat's PDF Writer. This "utility" creates a virtual printer for your documents. But instead of appearing on a virtual piece of paper, a PDF document is created.

The beauty of this method is that no conversion is needed before or after using PDF Writer; the PDF document is ready to be read by Acrobat Reader as soon as it is "printed."

Like other printers you can select (via the Chooser on Macintosh, or the Printer drop-down list on Windows), there are various options for the PDF Writer. Those options can be changed in the Page Setup (Macintosh) or Print Setup (Windows) dialog box in each application you print from.

Intro to PDF Writer

TM

PDF Writer acts like a printer connected to your Macintosh. You select it the same way you select a real printer—through the Chooser.

How to select PDF Writer on a Macintosh:

1. Select Chooser from the Apple menu. **Ⓐ**

2. Click on the Acrobat PDF Writer icon. **Ⓑ**

3. Close the Chooser Window. You'll be presented with a dialog box reminding you to check Page Setup in any applications. **Ⓒ**

4. Click OK to exit that box.

From this point forward, you'll be creating PDF files when you select Print from the File menu in any of your applications.

How to select a regular printer on a Macintosh:

1. Select Chooser from the Apple menu.

2. Click on the printer icon you'll be printing to. For instance, if you'll be printing on a LaserWriter, click the LaserWriter icon.

3. Click on your printer in the box on the right side of the Chooser window. You'll be presented with a dialog box reminding you to check Page Setup in any applications.

4. Click OK to exit that box.

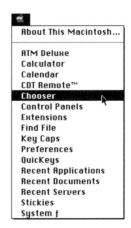

Ⓐ *Select Chooser from the Apple menu.*

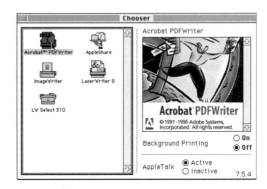

Ⓑ *Click on the Acrobat PDF Writer icon.*

Ⓒ *Click OK to exit the warning box.*

Using PDF Writer on a Macintosh

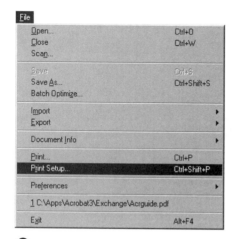

O *Select Print Setup from the File menu.*

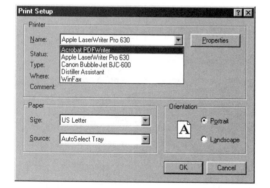

O *Select Acrobat PDF Writer from the Printer drop-down list.*

On a Windows system you select the PDF Writer just as you would select any other printer—from the Print Setup dialog box.

How to select PDF Writer on Windows:

1. Choose Print Setup from the File menu. **O**

2. Select Acrobat PDF Writer from the Printer drop-down list and click the OK button. **O**

From this point forward, you'll be creating PDF files when you select Print from the File menu in this application.

How to select a regular printer on Windows:

1. Choose Print Setup from the File menu.

2. Select the printer you'll be printing to from the Printer drop-down list and click the OK button.

Using PDF Writer on a Windows System

Creating a PDF file using the PDF Writer is very much like printing a document on a regular printer.

To print to the PDF Writer:

1. Select Print from the File menu.

2. Enter any options or changes in the Acrobat PDF Writer dialog box. **G**

3. If the options are correct, click the OK button to create the PDF file.

4. Enter any information you wish to change in the PDF Writer Document Information dialog box. **H**

5. Click the OK button.

6. Type in a new name for the PDF document when it is saved. **I**

7. Click the Save button.

The PDF file will be saved in the location you specified, and can be opened and viewed with either Acrobat Reader or Acrobat Exchange.

F *Choose Print from the File menu.*

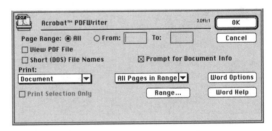

G *The Acrobat PDF Writer dialog box is similar to the Print dialog box.*

How to Print to the PDF Writer

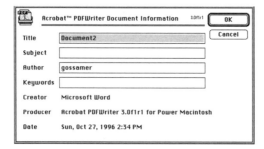

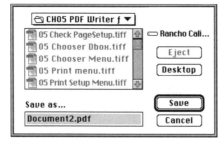

❶ *Make changes to the document information in this dialog box.*

❶ *Give the document a name and pick a save location for it before clicking the Save button.*

PDF Writer Options

There are several different options in the PDF Writer Dialog box. **❻** The options do the following:

Page Range controls the pages that are printed; either all the pages in the document or a range of pages specified in the From/To text fields.

View PDF File will automatically open the PDF file after it is created.

Short (DOS) File Names truncates the file name so that DOS systems (and Windows 3.1) can read the file name.

Prompt for Document Info displays a box which allows you to change information saved with the document.

PDF Writer Options

To change the PDF Writer options:

1. (Macintosh) Select Page Setup from the File menu.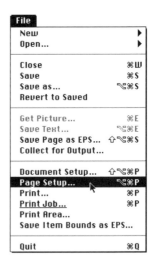

or

(Windows) Select Print Setup from the File menu, and click the Properties button.

2. Make any changes that need to be made in the Page Setup **K** or Properties dialog box.

3. Click OK when all changes have been made.

J *Choose Page Setup from the File menu.*

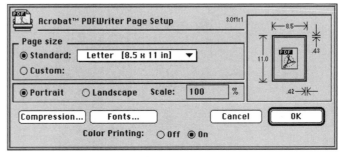

K *Make any changes needed in the Page Setup dialog box, then click the OK button.*

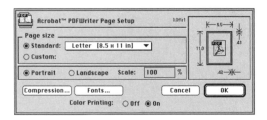

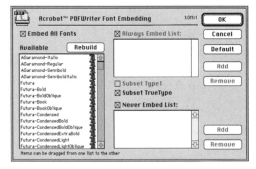

🄜 *Click the Fonts button in the Page Setup dialog box.*

🄜 *The Fonts dialog box allows you to specify which fonts will always be embedded and which ones will never be embedded.*

To embed fonts when printing via PDF Writer:

Fonts are normally embedded when printing to the PDF Writer. You can, however, change which fonts always embed and never embed in PDF Documents.

1. (Macintosh) Select Page Setup from the File menu.

   or

   (Windows) Select Print Setup from the File menu, and click the Properties button.

2. Click the Fonts button. 🄜

3. In the Font Embedding dialog box, select which fonts you would like to always have embedded in PDF files, and which fonts you never want to embed. 🄜

4. After all changes have been made, click the OK button.

5. Click the Page Setup or Properties OK button to return to the document.

How to Embed Fonts in PDF Documents

Acrobat Distiller can instantly change any PostScript file into a PDF document. PostScript files can be created directly from the Print dialog box of most applications.

The advantages of using Distiller (instead of PDF Writer) are that it provides a few more options than PDF Writer, it handles PostScript commands and objects better than PDF Writer, and PostScript code is less buggy than whatever an application initially spits out when printing.

Intro to Acrobat Distiller

TM

To create a PostScript file on a Macintosh:

1. Within any application, choose Print from the File menu.

2. Select the File option in the Print dialog box and click the Save button. **A**

3. Name the PostScript file and select a location for it.

A *Select the File radio button in the Print dialog box.*

To create a PostScript file with Windows:

1. Within any application, choose Print from the File menu.

2. Click the Print Setup button in the Print dialog box.

3. Click the Options button in the Print Setup dialog box.

4. Click the PostScript tab. **B**

5. Choose the Encapsulated PostScript (EPS) option. Click OK.

6. Click OK to exit the Print Setup dialog box. Click OK in the Print Document dialog box, and the PostScript file will be created.

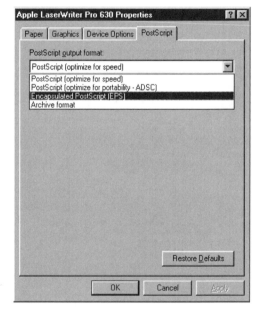

B *Select the EPS option in the PostScript tab of the Print Setup dialog box.*

Acrobat Distiller 3.0

G *Double-click on the Acrobat Distiller icon.*

Acrobat Distiller 3.0 has new compression capabilities which may produce PDF files not compatible with previous versions of Acrobat Exchange and Reader. To maintain compatibility, choose Acrobat 2.1; to take advantage of the new capabilities for smaller file sizes choose Acrobat 3.0. The setting may be changed later in the Distiller > Job Options dialog.

Please choose your default setting now.

[Acrobat 3.0]   [**Acrobat 2.1**]

D *Choose the version compatibility.*

To start Acrobat Distiller:

1. Double-click on the Acrobat Distiller icon. **G**

The first time you use Distiller, a compatibility dialog box will appear; you can choose between version 2.1 (which can be read by versions 2.1 and 3.0 of Acrobat Reader and Acrobat Exchange) and version 3.0 (which can only be read by version 3.0 of Acrobat Reader and Exchange). **D**

2. Choose the version you want to be compatible with (see the tip below for more details).

The main Acrobat Distiller window will appear in the center of your screen. **E**

Acrobat Distiller

Status: Ready
Size:
Source:

Percent Read: Page:

[Cancel Job] [Pause]

Messages

Acrobat Distiller 3.0b10 for Power Macintosh
Started: Friday, November 1, 1996 at 8:48 AM

PostScript® version: 2017.801

E *The Acrobat Distiller window.*

ACROBAT 3 TIP

There are very few instances when the Acrobat 2.1 format is needed. As time goes on, fewer and fewer people will still have Acrobat 2.1. Since Acrobat Reader 3.0 is free, take advantage of the extra compression that version 3.0 provides. You can always temporarily switch to version 2.1 in the Job Options dialog box.

Starting and Running Acrobat Distiller

To distill a PostScript file into a PDF file:

1. Choose Open from the File menu.

The Open dialog box will appear. **G**

2. Select the PostScript file you wish to distill and click the Open button.

The Save As dialog box will appear.

3. Name the file in the Save as: text field and click the Save button. **H**

The Acrobat Distiller window will show the progress of the distillation. **I**

F *Choose Open from the File menu.*

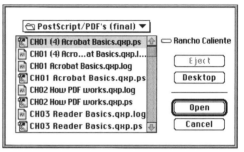

G *Select the file to distill.*

> **ACROBAT 3 TIP**
>
> You can quickly distill any PostScript file by dragging its icon on top of the Distiller icon. The file will be automatically saved in the same folder/directory of the original PostScript document and named with a .pdf extension.

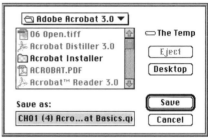

H *Name the file in the Save as: text field.*

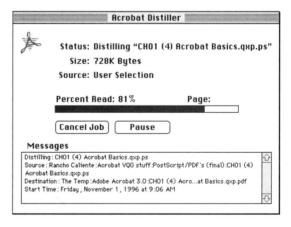

I *The progress bar shows the progress of the distillation.*

(side tab) **Distilling PostScript into PDF**

➊ *Choose Preferences from the Distiller menu.*

➋ *The Distiller Preferences dialog box.*

To change Distiller Preferences:

1. Choose Preferences from the Distiller menu. ➊

The Distiller Preferences dialog box will appear. ➋

2. Turn any options on and off by clicking on the checkboxes.

The three different options do the following:

Restart Distiller after PostScript fatal error. If Distiller reads code within a PostScript file that causes it to crash, it will automatically restart. This is a good option to have enabled when Distiller is being run from an unmanned server.

Notify if cannot connect to Watched Folder. If the Watched Folder is not available, a dialog box appears. Unless Distiller is being run on a server, it is a good idea to keep this option checked. Watched folders are discussed later in this chapter (page 64).

Display warning if startup volume is nearly full. Distiller uses the Startup volume as virtual memory while creating PDF files.

Acrobat Distiller Preferences

CHAPTER 6: USING ACROBAT DISTILLER

There are many more preferences in Acrobat Distiller than the tiny Preferences dialog box lets on. But instead of being labeled "preferences," they're called Job Options. These options affect the way each Distiller file is processed.

O *Choose Job Options from the Distiller menu.*

To change Distiller Job Options:

1. Choose Job Options from the Distiller menu. **O**

The Job Options dialog box will appear. **M**

2. Select the Job Options you wish to change.

General Job Options

Changing the Compatibility setting (from 3.0 to 2.1) will allow users of Acrobat 2.1 to open and modify PDF files. However, since Acrobat 3.0 Reader is free, and file sizes are substantially smaller, Acrobat 3.0 is usually the better choice.

The Default Resolution controls EPS image display. The Default Page Size controls the size of virtual paper the PDF file will appear on.

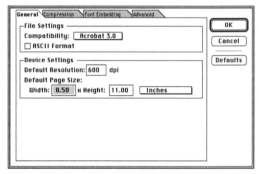

M *General Job Options.*

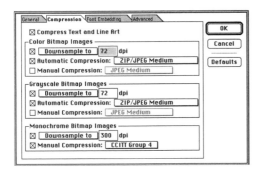

The Compression Job Options.

Compression Job Options

The Compress Text and Line Art control provides compression for black and white draw-based artwork. The three remaining options control how different image types are compressed.

Choosing downsample will reduce image resolution of those images to the dpi you specify.

Automatic or Manual Compression will apply the compression you specify. This compression is *lossy*, meaning that the images will lose information and possibly suffer image degradation.

Both Downsample and Automatic Compression are selected by default, and they are good options to use when you're pretty sure the PDF will be viewed only on screen.

Compression Job Options

Font Embedding Job Options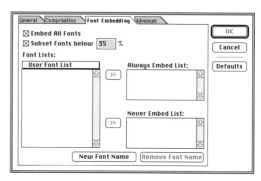

The Embed All Fonts option automatically embeds fonts, regardless of the contents of the Always Embed List or the Never Embed List.

The Subset option, when checked, looks at each font used in a document. If less than 35% of the characters in a font are used, only the characters used are embedded, not the entire font. This can substantially reduce the size of PDF files.

O *The Font Embedding Job Options.*

Advanced Job Options

The Advanced Job Options tab contains several settings that primarily apply if you plan on printing the PDF file at some point in the future.

The settings shown at right are the best choices to use when PDF files are to be displayed only on screen.

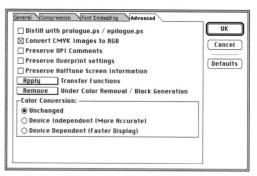

P *The Advanced Job Options.*

Font Embedding and Advanced Job Options

O *Select Font Locations from the Distiller menu.*

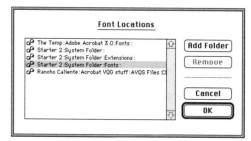

R *The Font Locations dialog box.*

Distiller looks for fonts in the standard font folder/directory. If you're using any font management software like ATM Deluxe, your fonts may reside in several different folders.

To change Distiller font locations:

1. Choose Font Locations from the Distiller menu. **O**

The Font Locations dialog box will appear. **R**

2. Remove any font locations by selecting the font to remove and clicking the Remove button.

3. Add an unlisted folder to the Font Locations list by clicking on the Add Folder button, and then selecting the folder to add.

The folder will appear in the Font Locations list.

Changing Acrobat Distiller Font Locations

Acrobat Distiller can be set up to automatically distill PostScript files into PDF files.

If your system is on a network with a server, the server is a perfect place to install and set up Distiller to automatically create PDF files from PostScript files. If you don't have a server, Acrobat can still automatically distill your files.

There are two steps to automating Distiller. First, the Distiller application must be running. Second, PostScript files need to be placed into a "watched" folder from which Distiller converts the files.

To make a Watched Folder:

1. In Distiller, choose Watched Folders from the Distiller menu. **S**

The Watched Folders dialog box will appear. **T**

2. Click the Add Folder button.

3. Select the folder that you wish Distiller to watch.

4. Click the OK button.

Whenever Distiller is running from this point forward, any PostScript files placed in the designated watched folder will be distilled into PDF files.

S Choose Watched Folders from the Distiller menu.

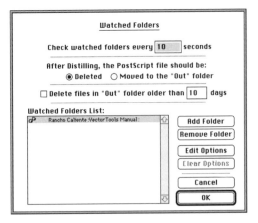

T The Watched Folders dialog box.

Automating Distiller with Watched Folders

7

You can use PDF files immediately after you create them, but there are all sorts of things that can be done to PDF files to make them more readable and easier to use. Acrobat Exchange provides several options for customizing PDF documents.

This chapter covers the changes you can make to PDF documents. Remember to save your documents after you've finished working with Acrobat Exchange so that other readers of your document will see the changes you've made. Choose Save from the File menu to save your changes to an open document, and the next time the document is opened, the changes will be there.

Intro to Acrobat Exchange

TM

To run Acrobat Exchange:

Locate the Acrobat Exchange icon and double-click on it. **A**

When Acrobat is loading, the Exchange screen will appear, and the plug-ins that are in the Exchange Plug-in folder will load. **B**

To quit Acrobat Exchange:

Select Quit from the File menu. **C**

Any open documents will be closed automatically. If changes to open documents were made, a dialog box will appear asking if you'd like to save those changes.

Acrobat™ Exchange 3.0

A Double-click on the Acrobat Exchange icon to run the program.

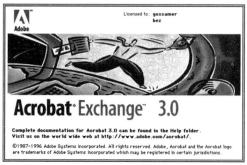

B The Exchange screen will appear while Exchange is starting up.

C Select Quit from the File menu to exit Exchange.

(vertical text) Running and Quitting Exchange

Choose Open from the File menu.

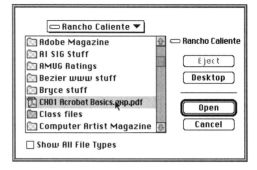

Select the file you want to open and click the Open button.

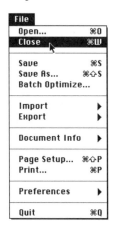

To close an open file, choose Close from the File menu.

To open a PDF file within Exchange:

1. Choose Open from the File menu. **D**

2. In the Open dialog box, select the PDF file you want to open and click the Open button. **E**

To open a PDF file from the Finder (Macintosh) or from the Windows desktop:

Drag the PDF file you would like to open on top of the Acrobat Exchange icon.

or

Double-click on the PDF File.

To close a PDF file:

Choose Close from the File menu. **F**

or

Click the close box on the document window.

Opening and Closing PDF Files with Exchange

To view Document Info:

Choose General from the Document Info submenu in the File menu. **G**

There is all sorts of information available in the General Info dialog box. Some of this information can be changed, while other parts of the information can't be modified. **H**

The items that can't be modified are:

Creator: This is the original application that created the original document from which the PDF file was created.

Producer: This is the software that was used to change the original document into a PDF document.

Created: This is the date that the PDF document was first created.

The items that can be modified, but not from the General Info dialog box:

Modified: The last time the PDF file was changed.

Optimized: If the file was set to be optimized (for the Web).

File Size: The size of the PDF file; this can change as the file is Modified or Optimized.

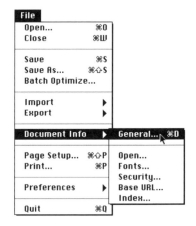

G *Choose General from the Document Info submenu.*

H *The General Info dialog box shows various information about the currently active PDF file.*

How to View Document Info

```
┌─────────────────────────────────────────────┐
│                 General Info                   │
├─────────────────────────────────────────────┤
│  Filename:  RAM Starter:Desktop Folder:CH12 Forms.pdf │
│                                                │
│     Title: │Chapter 12 Forms              │    │
│                                                │
│   Subject: │Forms/Acrobat VQE             │    │
│                                                │
│    Author: │Ted Alspach                   │    │
│                                                │
│  Keywords: │Forms Acrobat│                │    │
│                                                │
│    Creator:  Not Available                     │
│   Producer:  Acrobat Distiller 3.0 for Power Macintosh │
│                                                │
│    Created:  12/16/96 7:43:52 PM               │
│   Modified:  12/16/96 7:43:52 PM               │
│                                                │
│  Optimized:  No          File Size:  154463 Bytes │
│                                                │
│                        ┌────────┐ ┌──────────┐ │
│                        │ Cancel │ │    OK    │ │
│                        └────────┘ └──────────┘ │
└─────────────────────────────────────────────┘
```

❶ *In the General Info dialog box, the Title, Subject, Author, and Keywords can be modified.*

The only fields that can be changed in the General Info dialog box are the four at the top:

Title: The title of the document, but not necessarily the title of the file. Changing the file name has no effect on the title.

Subject: This is a descriptive category.

Author: This is the original author of the PDF files.

Keywords: These are words you can use for searches.

To change General Info:

1. Choose General from the Document Info submenu in the File menu.

2. Edit any of the text fields that can be edited (Title, Subject, Author, and Keywords). ❶

3. Click OK to make the changes.

4. Save the document by choosing Save from the File menu.

How to Change Document Info

By default, Acrobat Reader and Exchange open files to the first page, at the Fit Page zoom level. There may be times when you would like readers to open documents to a different page or zoom level.

To change the way files open:

1. Choose Open from the Document Info submenu in the File menu.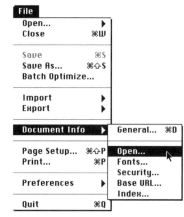

2. Make any changes in the Open Info dialog box.

Those options include the Initial View, which provides the choice of viewing just the page (Page Only), the bookmarks and page, or the thumbnails and page when the document is opened. You can set the page number the document will open to in the Page text field. Set the magnification in the Magnification text field. The Page Layout style (Default, Continuous, or Facing Pages) can be set here as well.

Window Options and User Interface Options are discussed on the next page.

3. Click the OK button.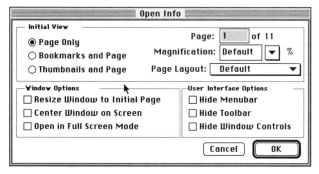

4. Save the document by choosing Save from the File menu.

The changes will appear the next time you open the document in either Acrobat Reader or Exchange.

J *Choose Open from the Document Info submenu.*

K *Click the OK button after changes have been made in the Open Info dialog box.*

L *Save the document after you've made your changes.*

Changing the way PDF Files Open

Open Info explanations

There are several things that can be changed in the Open Info dialog box besides the Initial View Options.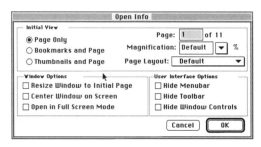

These include Window Options and User Interface Options.

Window Options

Resize Window to Initial Page looks at the magnification of the initial page when it is opened, and reduces the size of the surrounding window to match it.

Center Window on Screen places the window (at whatever size) in the center of your monitor when the document is opened.

Open in Full Screen Mode engages full screen mode, which hides the window edges, and appears to take over the entire screen.

User Interface Options

Hide Menubar hides the menu bar (until the cursor passes over the top of the screen).

Hide Toolbar hides the Acrobat toolbar from view.

Hide Window Controls removes the scrollbars, close, and resize boxes.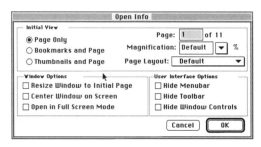

Ⓜ *Make changes in the Open Info dialog box.*

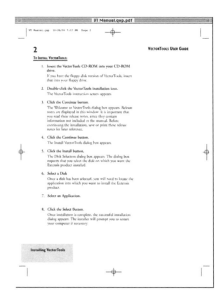

Ⓝ *A document set to open with Window Controls Hidden.*

Open Info Option Explanations

Occasionally, a PDF page will be rotated "the wrong way" when it is opened in Exchange. You can change the rotation in the Rotate Pages dialog box.

To rotate a PDF page:

1. Choose Rotate Pages from the Document menu. **O**

2. Select the direction you wish to rotate the pages in the Rotate Pages dialog box. Pages are rotated in 90° increments. **P**

3. Select which pages are to be rotated. To rotate several sets of non-contiguous pages, you'll have to do each contiguous set separately. For instance, to rotate pages 1, 2, 7, 8 and 9 of a 10-page document, you would have to rotate pages 1 and 2 first, then pages 7, 8, and 9.

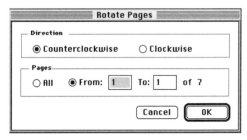

O *Choose Rotate Pages from the Document menu.*

P *Enter the direction and the number of pages to be rotated.*

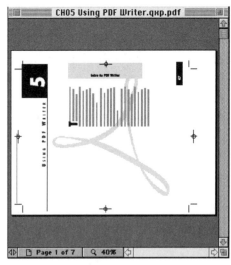

Q *The original document.*

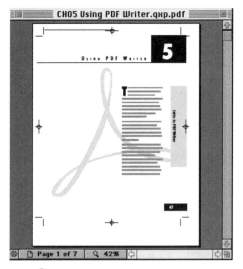

R *The document after being rotated 90° clockwise.*

Rotating PDF Pages

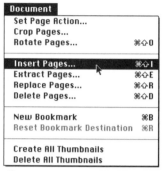

S *Choose Insert Pages from the Document menu.*

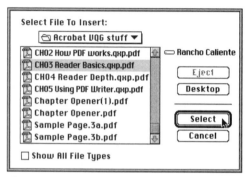

T *Select the file you wish to insert.*

Insert

Insert File: "CH03 Reader Basics.qxp.pdf"

— Location —
○ Before ● After

— Page —
○ First   ○ Last   ● Page : [1]   of 7

[Cancel] [OK]

U *Select where the pages are to be inserted.*

There really isn't a "merge" feature in Acrobat Exchange, but you do have the ability to add other PDF documents to the current, "active" PDF document.

To insert pages into a PDF document:

1. Choose Insert Pages from the Document menu. **S**

2. In the Select File To Insert dialog box, find the file you'd like to insert into the current document. When the file is located, click the Select button. **T**

3. Indicate the location (Before or After) and the page you want to insert, then click the OK button. **U**

The pages will be inserted at the document location you have selected.

> If you don't want the contents of an entire PDF file to be inserted, you'll have to open that PDF file and extract the pages you want to insert. This can get confusing, so be sure to distinctly name the extracted pages of the document. Extracting pages is explained on the following page.
>
> **ACROBAT 3 TIP**

Inserting Pages

Selected pages from within PDF Documents can be exported (Acrobat calls this extracting) into a new document. The extraction process can also be used to remove pages at the same time; this, in effect, can break a PDF document into smaller documents.

To extract a page from a PDF document:

1. Choose Extract Pages from the Document menu.

2. Enter the page (or pages) you wish to extract in the Extract Pages dialog box. **W**

3. If you want the extracted pages deleted from the current document, check the Delete Pages After Extracting checkbox.

4. Click the OK button.

The pages will be extracted into a new, open document. This document is *not* saved, so be sure to save the document before closing it. **X**

V *Choose Extract Pages from the Document menu.*

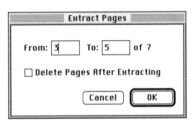

W *Enter the page range of pages to be extracted.*

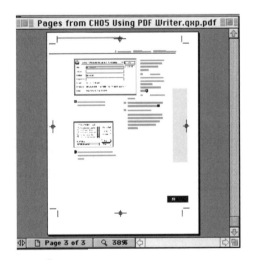

X *The document that has been extracted will appear in Acrobat Exchange as the current, active document.*

Extracting PDF Pages

Choose Replace Pages from the Document menu.

Document	
Set Page Action...	
Crop Pages...	
Rotate Pages...	⌘⇧0
Insert Pages...	⌘⇧I
Extract Pages...	⌘⇧E
Replace Pages...	⌘⇧R
Delete Pages...	⌘⇧D
New Bookmark	⌘B
Reset Bookmark Destination	⌘R
Create All Thumbnails	
Delete All Thumbnails	

ⓨ *Choose Replace Pages from the Document menu.*

Select File With New Pages:

📁 Acrobat UQG stuff ▼

- 📄 CH02 How PDF works.qxp.pdf
- 📄 CH03 Reader Basics.qxp.pdf
- 📄 CH04 Reader Depth.qxp.pdf
- 📄 CH05 Using PDF Writer.qxp.pdf
- 📄 Chapter Opener(1).pdf
- 📄 Chapter Opener.pdf
- 📄 Sample Page.3a.pdf
- 📄 Sample Page.3b.pdf

☐ Show All File Types

▭ Rancho Caliente

[Eject]
[Desktop]
[Select]
[Cancel]

ⓩ *Select the file that contains the replacement pages.*

═ Replace Pages ═

┌─ Original ────────────────────────
│ Replace Pages: [1] To: [1] of 7
│ in "CH05 Using PDF Writer.qxp.pdf"
└────────────────────────────────────

┌─ Replacement ─────────────────────
│ With Pages: [1] To: 1 of 5
│ from "CH02 How PDF works.qxp.pdf"
└────────────────────────────────────

[Cancel] [OK]

ⓐⓐ *Select the page range to be replaced, as well as the page range that will replace it.*

Acrobat Exchange allows you to replace a page with a PDF page from another document. This is very useful when using Adobe Illustrator (see Chapter 10) to edit individual pages of a PDF document.

To replace a page with another page:

1. Choose Replace Pages from the Document menu. **ⓨ**

2. Select the file that contains the replacement pages and click the Select button. **ⓩ**

3. In the Replace Pages dialog box, enter the pages to be replaced in the Original box. **ⓐⓐ**

4. Enter the replacement pages in the Replacement box.

5. Click the OK button, and your original pages will be replaced.

Replacing PDF Pages

> You can replace any number of pages with any other number of pages. For instance, you can replace pages 4-6 in your open document with pages 11-26 from another document. The current document will then be 13 pages longer than it was before you replaced those pages.
>
> **ACROBAT 3 TIP**

Pages created by different applications may contain extra areas that you don't need. Acrobat Exchange provides a way to crop out the unneeded areas.

To crop a PDF page:

1. Choose Crop Pages from the Document menu. **BB** The Crop Pages dialog box will appear.

2. Enter the distance from each edge that you wish to crop the page. **CC**

As you change the numbers (either by typing in new values or by clicking the arrows), a dotted line will appear on each of the margins you are cropping. These dotted lines show where the actual edges of the cropped page will be. **DD**

3. Enter the page range to crop. To crop all the pages in a document, choose the All radio button.

4. Click the OK button.

A message will appear asking if you really want to crop the selected pages.

BB *Choose Crop Pages from the Document menu.*

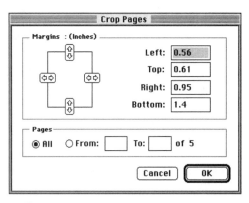

CC *Enter where the crops will be and what pages they will affect.*

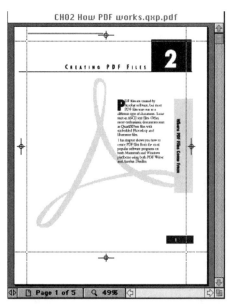

DD *Dotted lines show where cropping will take place.*

Cropping PDF Pages

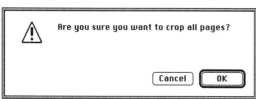

Are you sure you want to crop all pages?

Cancel   OK

EE *Click OK if you're sure you want to crop the pages.*

5. Click OK to crop the pages as you've indicated, or click the Cancel button to leave the document untouched. **EE**

The pages will be cropped. **GG** You can undo this action by pressing Command-Z (Macintosh) or Control-Z (Windows). **FF**

If you save and reopen the document at a later time, there is no way to retrieve the areas that have been cropped.

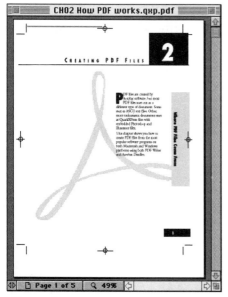

FF *The page before cropping.*

GG *The page after cropping.*

Cropping PDF Pages

Extracting removes pages from a PDF document, but it also creates a new document with the extracted pages. Sometimes you just want to get rid of certain pages. Acrobat Exchange does this with the Delete function.

To delete a page from a PDF document:

1. Choose Delete Pages from the Document menu.  The Delete Pages dialog box will appear.

2. Enter the page range you wish to delete in the Delete Pages dialog box. **①**

3. Click OK to delete the pages you've specified.

When you do this, a dialog box will appear asking if you're sure you want to delete the specified pages. **①**

4. If you are sure, click the OK button. If not, click the Cancel button.

Choose Delete Pages from the Document menu.

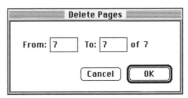

① *Enter the page range you wish to delete.*

① *Click OK if you're sure you want to delete the indicated page(s).*

Deleting Pages from PDF Documents

Acrobat Exchange has a multitude of advanced options that make PDF files easier to use and read.

These features include bookmarks, thumbnails, notes, and text editing capabilities.

All sorts of other things can be added to PDF documents as well, including links to other locations (including Web pages), and even movies!

Exchange is a huge piece of software. While I'll cover much of what it does in this and the previous chapter, Exchange still has many other capabilities. Those features, such as Links, forms, and using the Web with PDF documents are discussed in additional chapters devoted to those specific topics.

Acrobat Exchange in Depth

Bookmarks are commonly used within PDF files to quickly go to a specific location (page and zoom level) within a PDF document. Bookmarks can do many other things as well, as you'll see on the next few pages.

To create a bookmark:

1. Go to a page and zoom to where you want the bookmark to go.

2. Choose New Bookmark from the Document menu. **Ⓐ**

A new bookmark will appear to the left of the document in Bookmark view. If you weren't already in Bookmark view, Acrobat changes to this view automatically.

The bookmark is named Untitled, but the name can easily be changed. **Ⓑ**

3. Type the name of the bookmark. Its name could be a description of its location or the page's topic.

Press Return after you've type the name, and the bookmark will be ready to use. **Ⓒ**

Ⓐ *Choose New Bookmark from the Document menu.*

Ⓑ *By default, a new bookmark is named Untitled. It is highlighted so that you can change the name by simply typing.*

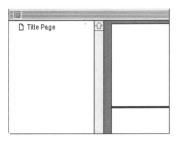

Ⓒ *After its name is changed, the bookmark is no longer highlighted.*

If you switch from Bookmark view back to Page Only view, the bookmark will still be in place, it just won't be visible. The next time you enter Bookmark view, the bookmark(s) you've created will appear.

ACROBAT 3 TIP

Creating Bookmarks

⓪ *Change to Bookmark view by choosing Bookmarks and Page from the View menu.*

⓮ *Select a bookmark by clicking on the icon to the left of the bookmark.*

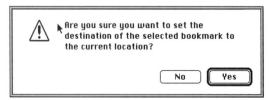

⓯ *Choose Reset Bookmark Destination from the Document menu.*

To view a bookmark:

1. Choose Bookmarks and Page from the View menu. **⓪**

2. Click on the bookmark you wish to view.

The screen will change to show the location of that bookmark.

To change the location of a bookmark:

1. Select the bookmark you wish to modify by clicking on the bookmark icon. **⓮**

2. Move to the intended target location in the document.

3. Choose Reset Bookmark Destination from the Document menu. **⓯**

4. Click Yes in the warning dialog box to reset the bookmark. **⓰**

Viewing and Relocating Bookmarks

Are you sure you want to set the destination of the selected bookmark to the current location?

[No]   [**Yes**]

⓰ *Click Yes to reset the bookmark's destination.*

To change a bookmark's properties:

1. Select the bookmark by clicking on its icon.

2. Choose Properties from the Edit menu. **ⓗ**

The Bookmark Properties palette will appear. **ⓘ**

3. Choose the type of action from the Type pop-up menu. **ⓙ**

4. If you want to change the Destination as well as the type, click the Edit Destination button in the Properties palette.

5. Change the location of the bookmark by moving the page around until the bookmark is where you want it.

6. To change the Magnification setting, select a different setting from the Magnification pop-up menu. **ⓚ**

7. Click the OK button on the Bookmark Properties palette.

ⓗ *After the bookmark is selected, choose Properties from the Edit menu.*

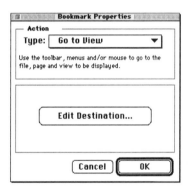

ⓘ *The Bookmark Properties palette.*

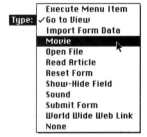

ⓙ *Change the Action type by choosing an action from the Type pop-up menu.*

ⓚ *Change the magnification by clicking the Edit Destination button, and then choose a new magnification from the Magnification pop-up menu.*

Changing Bookmark Properties

82

❶ *Move a bookmark by clicking on it and dragging it up or down within the list.*

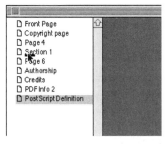

ⓜ *Embed a bookmark by dragging it up or down within the list and to the right of the icon you wish to embed it within.*

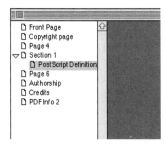

ⓝ *When a bookmark is embedded, it appears under and indented from the original bookmark.*

By default, bookmarks appear in the order in which you create them. However, you might want to change that order, or change the long list into a more useful hierarchical approach. For instance, you may want a section page to be a main category, while a chapter opener would be a subcategory.

To change the placement of a bookmark within the list:

1. Select the bookmark to be moved by clicking on its icon.

2. Drag the bookmark up or down within the list. A black line will appear under the icon of a bookmark showing you where the dragged bookmark will be moved. **❶**

3. Release the mouse button.

To move a bookmark so that it is embedded hierarchically within another bookmark:

1. Select the bookmark to be embedded by clicking on its icon.

2. Drag the bookmark up or down within the list just to the right of the icon in which you want to embed it. A black line will appear under the name of a bookmark showing where the dragged bookmark will be moved. **ⓜ**

3. Release the mouse button.

The dragged bookmark is now "embedded" within the bookmark it was dragged on top of. **ⓝ**

Moving and Embedding Bookmarks

Thumbnails provide a quick and easy method to go to another page. Each thumbnail is a tiny representation of each page. Clicking on a thumbnail instantly takes you to that page at the current magnification level.

To create thumbnails for the current document:

Choose Create All Thumbnails from the Document menu. ❶

Thumbnails for the document will be created and displayed to the left of the document.

To view and use thumbnails in the current document:

1. Choose Thumbnails and Page from the View Menu.

Thumbnails for the document will be displayed to the left of the document. ❷

2. Click on the thumbnail that represents the page you wish to go to.

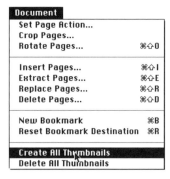

❶ *Choose Create All Thumbnails from the Document menu.*

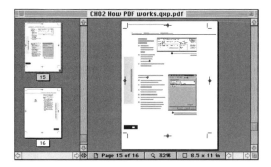

❷ *Thumbnails are shown to the left of the document.*

Creating and Viewing Thumbnails

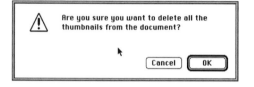

O *Choose Delete All Thumbnails from the Document menu.*

R *Click OK in the warning dialog box to delete the pages.*

To delete thumbnails from the current document:

1. Choose Delete All Thumbnails from the Document menu. **O**

2. Click the OK button in the "Are you sure?" dialog box that appears. **R**

The document will return to Page Only view and the thumbnails will be deleted.

To change thumbnails to reflect editing done within Acrobat:

1. Choose Delete All Thumbnails from the Document menu.

2. Click the OK button in the "Are you sure?" dialog box that appears.

The document will return to Page Only view and the thumbnails will be deleted.

3. Choose Create All Thumbnails from the Document menu.

New, updated thumbnails for the document will be created and displayed to the left of the document.

Deleting and Changing Thumbnails

Notes can add a comment or thought to a page or area upon a page in a PDF document. Notes are unobtrusive and are only display when double-clicked.

To create a note:

1. Choose Note from the Tools menu. **S**

The Note tool will now be selected.

2. Create a note by dragging on a document page. The size of the rectangle created by the drag will be the size of the note. **T**

The note can be resized at any time after it is created.

Once the mouse button is released, the note will appear on the page. **U**

Type any desired text into the newly-created note.

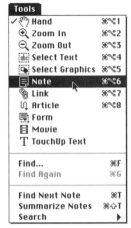

S *Choose Note from the Tools menu.*

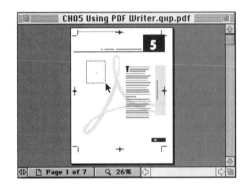

T *Drag with the Note tool to create a note.*

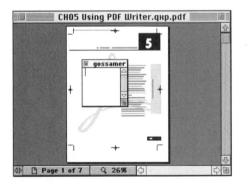

U *The note will appear on the page.*

Creating a Note

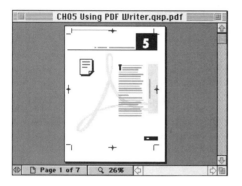

V *Double-click on the note to edit the text within it.*

To add text to an existing note:

1. Double-click on the note that you want to add text to. *V*

The note will open up, allowing you to type in text.

2. Type in the text you want to enter. *W*

3. To close the note, click in the close box of the note window (in the upper-left corner of the note).

> You can resize a note window by dragging the lower-right corner. The note will default to that new size when it is opened next.
>
> **ACROBAT 3 TIP**

W *Type within the note. Resize the note by clicking and dragging in the lower right corner.*

Adding Text to a Note

To import notes:

1. Choose Notes from the Import submenu under the File menu. **ⓧ**

2. From the Import Notes dialog box, select the file that contains the notes you wish to import. **ⓨ**

You can import notes from any other PDF document which contains them.

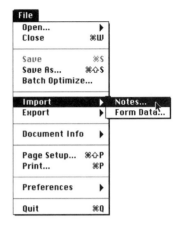

ⓧ *Choose Notes from the Import submenu.*

Importing Notes

> Imported notes always appear on their original page numbers. So if a note was on page 3 of the imported document, it will appear on page 3 of the document it is imported into. If there was no page 3 in the current document, a page 3 will be created, and will contain just the note on that page.

ACROBAT 3 TIP

Select File Containing Notes:

📁 PostScript/PDF's (final) ▼

📄 CH01 (4) Acro...at Basics.qxp....
📄 CH01 Acrobat Basics.qxp.pdf
📄 CH02 How PDF works.qxp.pdf
📄 CH03 Reader Basics.qxp.pdf
📄 CH04 Reader Depth.qxp.pdf
📄 CH05 Using PDF Writer.qxp.pdf

⬜ Rancho Caliente

[Eject]
[Desktop]

[Select]
[Cancel]

☐ Show All File Types

ⓨ *Select the file that contains the notes you wish to import.*

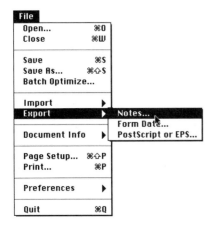

⓿ *Choose Notes from the Export submenu.*

To export notes:

1. Choose Notes from the Export submenu. **⓿**

2. Name the file you wish to export the notes into. **⓪**

A new PDF file is created. The notes will be saved as a PDF document with only the notes on the pages.

All the pages in the PDF document are exported as "empty," with no text or graphics on them at all.

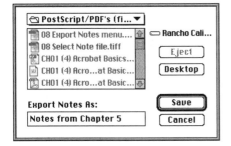

⓪ *Name the file you wish to export the notes to.*

Exporting Notes

89

To delete existing notes:

1. Click on the note you wish to delete.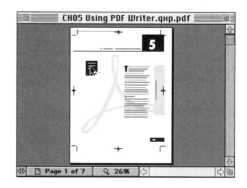

2. Press the Delete key.

3. Click OK in the "Are You Sure" dialog box. ⓒⓒ

ⓑⓑ *Click on the Note you wish to Delete.*

ⓒⓒ *Click OK to delete the note.*

Deleting Notes

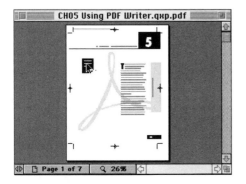

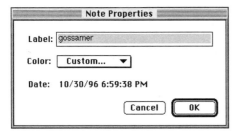

DD *Click on the note you want to change.*

EE *Select the new color from the pull-down menu.*

You can specify the color of notes to be one of several different colors. This is a function of pure preference; the colors don't mean anything to the note.

To change the color of a note:

1. Select the note you wish to change by clicking on it once. **DD**

2. Select Properties from the Edit menu.

3. In the Note Properties dialog box, select the color for the note from the Color pop-up menu. **EE**

4. Click the OK button to change the color of the note.

Changing Note Color

Editing Text with Acrobat Exchange

To edit text within Acrobat Exchange:

1. Choose TouchUp Text from the Tools menu. **Ⓕ**

2. Click on any text in the PDF document.

3. Select text by dragging across it. **ⒼⒼ**

4. Replace selected text by typing.

To move text within Acrobat Exchange:

1. Choose TouchUp Text from the Tools menu.

2. Click on any text in the PDF document. Triangles appear to the left of thetext.

3. Move the text by clicking on the triangles to the left of that text and dragging. **ⒽⒽ**

To delete text within Acrobat Exchange:

1. Choose TouchUp Text from the Tools menu.

2. Click on any text in the PDF document.

3. Select text by dragging across it.

4. Press the Delete key.

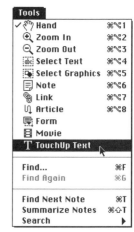

Ⓕ *Choose TouchUp Text from the Tools menu.*

CH05 Using PDF Writer.qxp.pdf

PTER 5: USING PDF W

PDF Writer acts like a printer connected to your Macintosh. You select it the same way you select a re printer—through the Chooser.

ⒼⒼ *Select text by dragging across it.*

CH05 Using PDF Writer.qxp.pdf

PTER 5: USING PDF W

PDF Writer acts like a printer connected to your Macintosh. You select it the same way y printer—through the Chooser.

ⒽⒽ *Move a text block by dragging the triangles at the left of the text.*

Double-clicking on text will select one word at a time. Clicking three times will select an entire row of text.

ACROBAT 3 TIP

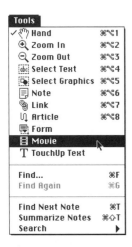

To add movies to a PDF Document:

1. Choose Movie from the Tools menu.

2. Drag a rectangle to indicate the size and location where you'd like a movie to be placed. **JJ**

3. Select a movie from the Open Movie dialog box.

After the movie has been selected, the Movie Properties dialog box will appear.

4. Enter any changes to the way the movie will open and play, and then click OK. **KK**

II *Choose Movie from the Tools menu.*

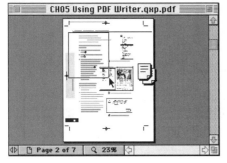

JJ *Drag a rectangle to define the size and location of the movie.*

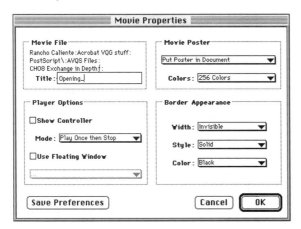

KK *Set the way the movie opens and plays.*

Adding Movies to PDF Documents

Articles allow readers to follow stories easily in PDF documents.

To create an article:

1. Choose Article from the Tools menu.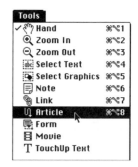

2. With the Article tool, click and drag around the first section of the text you want to define as part of an article.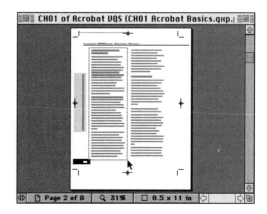

When the mouse button is released, the article will be surrounded by a four-cornered box and numbered, using the scheme 1-1, where the first number is the number of the article, and the second number is the part of that article.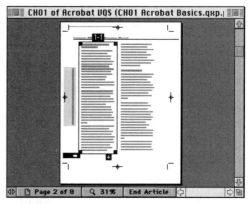

Clicking on another tool will end the article, and display the Article Properties dialog box. **PP**

LL *Choose Article from the Tools menu.*

MM *Drag around the first portion of the article.*

NN *The article is indicated by a cornered box and is numbered at the top of that box.*

Creating Articles

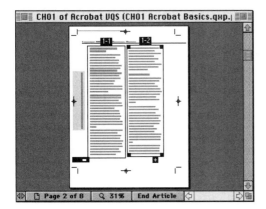

Linked articles share the same first number; second numbers follow in succession.

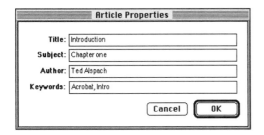

After an article has been created, information can be added to the Article Properties dialog box.

After the first part of an article has been defined, the article can be continued to other pages or sections of text.

To continue an article:

1. Click on the original article with the article tool.

2. Drag around the next article you want linked to the first one.

The next section of the article will continue with the second part of the number following the first article.

For instance, if there were three parts to article number 1, the parts would be defined as 1-1, 1-2, and 1-3.

Clicking on another tool will end the article, and display the Article Properties dialog box.

Continuing Articles and Article Properties

This chapter is probably as close as I'll ever get to giving golf advice, much to the appreciation of the PGA. Links in Acrobat work much like my own personal golf game: Acrobat has the ability to instantly go to any other location, whether on the same page, the same document, a different document, or even on the World Wide Web. Likewise, any golf ball I hit has a propensity to go not only anywhere on the same fairway, but could also end up anywhere on the same course, a different course, or (considering all the balls I've lost) another dimension entirely.

Acrobat Exchange provides the tools to create links that give users one click access to other locations.

Links

How links work

Links provide a convenient way to navigate PDF documents. By clicking on a certain area right on the page (no bookmarks needed), the person viewing the PDF document is instantly taken to another location.

Links can be made very obvious, or they can be hidden within the document, appearing only when your cursor passes over the link.

To use a link:

Click on the link that you wish to use. **A**

The document will instantly change views to show the new location. **B**

A *Click on a link in a PDF document.*

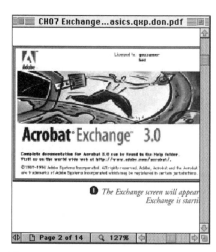

B *After clicking, the document will display the linked location.*

> You can still detect a link in a PDF document, even if it isn't displayed with an outline. When your cursor passes over the link, it will change into a pointing finger.
>
> **ACROBAT 3 TIP**

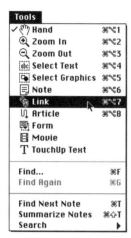

O *Choose Link from the Tools menu.*

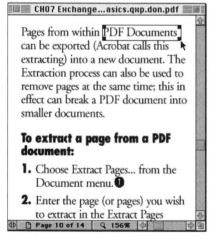

O *Drag around the area that will make up the link.*

To create a link from one spot in a PDF document to another spot:

1. Choose Link from the Tools menu. **O**

2. Drag around the area you wish to define as a link. **O**

When you release the mouse button, the Link Properties palette will appear. You might want to move this out of your way (but don't close it) when setting the location of the link.

3. Using Acrobat's tools, move to the page and zoom level where you want the link to go.

4. Click OK in the Link Properties palette. **O**

The link will work whenever the Hand tool is active. Test it by clicking on the link with the Hand tool.

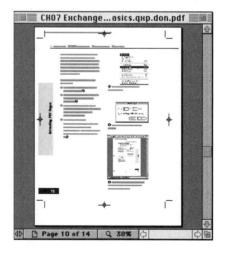

O *Before clicking OK in the Link Properties palette, set the page and size you wish to be at when the link is activated.*

Creating Links within Acrobat Exchange

To change zoom levels using a link:

1. Choose Link from the Tools menu.

2. Drag around the area you wish to define as a zoom link.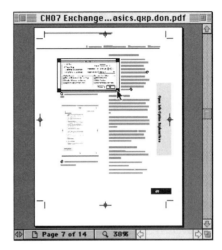

When you release the mouse button, the Link Properties palette will appear. You might want to move this out of your way (but don't close it) when setting the zoom level of the link.

3. Using the Zoom tool, zoom into the page where you want the link to zoom to. **G**

4. Click OK in the Create Links palette.

The zoom level will change whenever you have the Hand tool and click on the link.

To edit an existing link:

1. Choose Link from the Tools menu.

2. Double-click on an existing link.

The link corners will be displayed along with the Link Properties palette.

3. Change the location or zoom level for the link.

4. Click the OK button in the Link Properties palette.

F *Draw a rectangle around the area you'd like to use as a zoom link.*

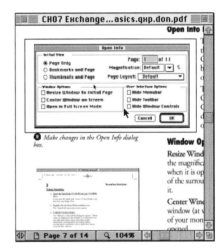

G *The zoomed-in view.*

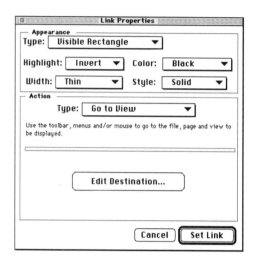

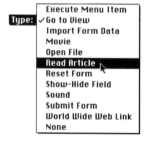

H *Many different properties can be changed in the Link Properties palette.*

O *The different types of actions that can be assigned to a link.*

To edit the properties of a link:

1. Choose Link from the Tools menu.

2. Double-click on an existing link.

The link corners will be displayed along with the Link Properties palette. **H**

3. Change any of the properties using the Type pop-up menu in the Link Properties palette. **O**

4. Click the OK button in the Link Properties palette.

Link Properties

To delete a link:

1. Choose Link from the Tools menu.

2. Click once on an existing link.

The link corners will be displayed.

3. Press the Delete key.

A box will appear asking if you really want to remove the link from the document.

4. Click the OK button. **J**

The link will be removed.

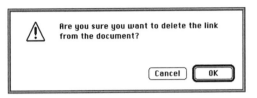

J *Click OK to delete the link.*

Deleting Links

Adobe Illustrator is the best tool that you can use to edit PDF files. Illustrator is the only application that can process the multitude of graphics types and text controls that Acrobat can edit, and is thus perfect to use as a complete editing tool.

Unfortunately, at the time of this writing (late 1996), Adobe has not yet released a current version of Adobe Illustrator for Windows that opens PDF files. Current version 4.1 will not open PDF files. Adobe is said to be hard at work on a new version of the software for Macintosh and Windows for release sometime in 1997. At that time, this chapter should apply to both platforms, but right now it only applies to Macintosh owners.

Using Adobe Illustrator to Edit PDF Files

TM

To open a PDF file in Illustrator:

1. Choose Open from the File menu.  **Ⓐ**

2. Select the PDF file from the Open dialog box and click the Open button. **Ⓑ**

The Page Selection dialog box will appear. **Ⓒ**

3. In the Page Selection dialog box, select the page you wish to open and click OK. This box will not appear if the PDF file contains only one page. Thumbnails are only present if they have been created within Exchange.

The document page will appear in Illustrator. **Ⓓ**

Ⓐ *Choose Open from Illustrator's File menu.*

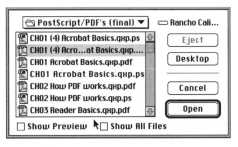

Ⓑ *Select the PDF file you wish to open.*

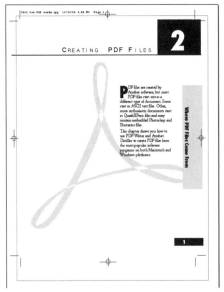

Ⓓ *The PDF Document shown in Illustrator.*

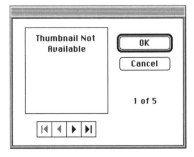

Ⓒ *The Page Selection dialog box.*

To edit text of a PDF file in Illustrator:

1. Select the Type tool from the Illustrator Toolbox. **E**

2. Click in the area of the PDF page you wish to edit.

3. Drag to select text. **F**

4. Type to replace selected text. **G**

E *Select the Type tool in the Illustrator toolbox.*

PDF files are created by Acrobat software, but most PDF files start out as a different type of document. Some start as ASCII text files. Other, more enthusiastic documents start as QuarkXPress files and may contain embedded Photoshop and Illustrator files.

F *Select text by dragging the Type tool through the text.*

PDF files are created by Acrobat software, but most PDF files start out as a different type of document. Some start as monsters from outer space. A few begin their hopeless lives as low level viruses. A few begin as cheese and Illustrator files.

G *Type new text to replace the highlighted text.*

Editing PDF Text in Illustrator

PDF files may contain artwork in two different formats.

Pixel-based. These include photographs, scans, and images created in applications like Photoshop or Painter. These images can be moved, scaled, rotated, sheared, and flipped within Illustrator.

Vector-based. These include images created with draw and PostScript software, such as ClarisDraw and Adobe Illustrator. Also, most objects created in page layout software are vector-based. These images can be completely modified, in addition to being transformed in the same ways as pixel-based images.

To edit an image within Illustrator:

1. Choose the Selection tool (solid arrow) from the Illustrator toolbox. **H**

2. Select the object or objects you wish to edit. **I**

3. Select the tool or command to edit the selected image. **J**

H *Choose the Selection tool in the toolbox.*

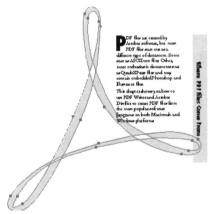

I *Select the object by clicking it.*

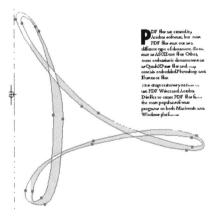

J *The object after modification.*

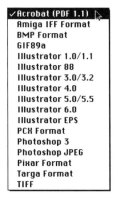

Ⓚ *Choose Save from the File menu.*

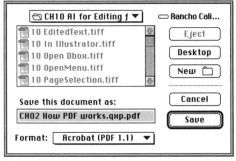

Ⓛ *The Save As dialog box.*

Ⓜ *Choose the Acrobat PDF format from the pop-up menu.*

Any file that can be opened in Illustrator can be saved as a PDF file, whether the file was created in Illustrator or originally as a PDF file.

To save a PDF file within Illustrator:

1. Choose Save from the File menu. **Ⓚ**

The Save As dialog box will appear. **Ⓛ**

2. Name the file and choose a location.

3. Choose Acrobat PDF format from the Format pop-up menu. **Ⓜ**

4. Click the Save button.

Saving PDF Files in Illustrator

Plug-ins can add a variety of functions and features to Acrobat. Some plug-ins are designed to help you create and modify PDF files within Exchange, while others provide special viewing capabilities within Reader.

Many plug-ins are available free from the Web or directly from Adobe. Other plug-ins can be purchased from a variety of plug-in manufacturers.

The best thing about plug-ins is that while they add functionality to Acrobat, they don't change the fundamental way the software works. So it doesn't matter if a PDF file was created with "Joe's Amazing Acrobat Plug-ins" because you can still view that file, even if you don't have those plug-ins.

Plug-ins

TM

How plug-ins work in Acrobat

A plug-in is just a file that Acrobat Exchange (or Reader) recognizes and loads. Within that file is the programming code that creates additional functions.

Acrobat always looks to the Plug-Ins folder located in the Acrobat folder. **Ⓐ** If it finds plug-ins in that folder, they are automatically loaded into Acrobat, and any features associated with them are added when appropriate.

Plug-ins can add tools, menu items, and floating palettes to the Acrobat interface. Adobe provides a special kit to anyone who is interested in creating plug-ins for Acrobat.

Using plug-ins in Acrobat

Because most plug-ins for Acrobat simply add to the feature list of the product, using new plug-ins is as simple as choosing a menu item, using a tool, or clicking somewhere on a floating palette.

Many plug-ins come with an installer. However, individual plug-ins you may download can often consist simply of the plug-in file itself.

To install new plug-ins:

1. Drag the plug-in from its current location into the Acrobat Plug-Ins folder.

2. Double-click on the Acrobat program icon.

The plug-in will load automatically.

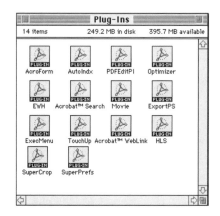

Ⓐ *The Acrobat Plug-Ins folder.*

How Plug-ins Work

110

The Super Crop plug-in

One of Adobe's free plug-ins for Acrobat Exchange is called Super Crop. Super Crop provides a cropping tool that is easier to use than the standard cropping function within Acrobat.

Install the Super Crop Plug-in by dragging it into your Acrobat Plug-Ins folder.

To crop with the Super Crop tool:

1. Select Super Crop from the Tools menu. ❸ The cursor will change into a little cropping tool (that's what that funny shape is supposed to be, anyway).

2. Click and drag across the area that you want to *keep* in the PDF file. When you release the mouse button, a box with four handled corners will appear.

3. Click on one of the handles and drag to adjust the cropping area. Remember that the Super Crop tool crops away everything that is outside of the rectangle you're adjusting.

4. When you've finished adjusting, click in the middle of the rectangle. A dialog box will appear, asking if you would like to crop the current page, all the pages, or if you wish to cancel.

5. Click either All or Current. The page(s) will be cropped as you've specified.

6. Save the document.

❸ *Select Super Crop from the Tools menu.*

One of the drawbacks to using Super Crop vs. Acrobat's built-in cropping function is that cropping can't be specified numerically; only by appearance on the page. Because of this, it is usually a good idea to use Super Crop at the largest magnification possible.

ACROBAT 3 TIP

Using the Super Crop Plug-in

The Super Preferences plug-in

Another free plug-in from Adobe is Super Preferences. Super Preferences adds functionality to the current set of preferences by providing a hot list of documents, automatic tiling of documents, and other options.

Install the Super Preferences plug-in by dragging it into the Acrobat Plug-Ins folder.

To Use the Super Preferences plug-in:

1. Choose Super Preferences from the Preferences submenu in the File menu. **C** The Super Preferences dialog box will appear. **D**

2. Select or deselect the options you desire.

3. Click the OK button when you've finished.

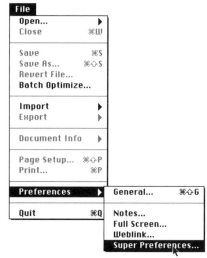

C *Choose Super Preferences from the Preferences submenu of the File menu.*

The Super Preferences Options

File Open Behavior provides the ability to open more than one document at a time, and to be able to switch between them with a click of a button on the toolbar.

Hot List is a new menu added to the Acrobat menu bar. You can add PDF documents to this list for easy opening at a later time.

AutoTiling automatically tiles documents when more than one are opened.

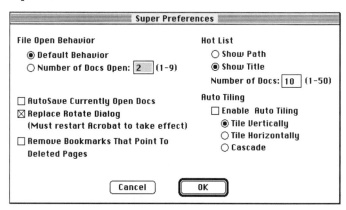

D *The Super Preferences dialog box provides many more preference options than are found in Acrobat's standard preferences.*

Using the Super Preferences Plug-in

Using third-party plug-ins in Acrobat

Many companies are providing third-party plug-ins for Adobe Acrobat that enhance its functionality in some way.

Adobe maintains a list of all the current Acrobat plug-ins that are available on its Web site at http://www.adobe.com.

At the time of this writing (at the completion of version 3 of Acrobat), there were no plug-ins that took advantage of Acrobat 3.0's new features. Many companies had announced products, but they were several months from shipping.

12

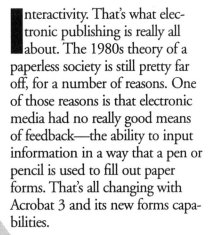

Interactivity. That's what electronic publishing is really all about. The 1980s theory of a paperless society is still pretty far off, for a number of reasons. One of those reasons is that electronic media had no really good means of feedback—the ability to input information in a way that a pen or pencil is used to fill out paper forms. That's all changing with Acrobat 3 and its new forms capabilities.

Forms allow individuals who view a document with Acrobat Reader to fill in text fields, choose options, click buttons, and even send information automatically over the Internet.

Setting up forms is designed to be as simple as possible, with a straightforward list of options and a single Form tool to assist you.

About Forms

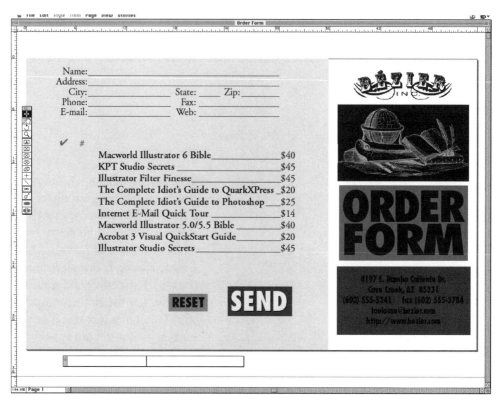

A form document is simply a PDF file to which you can add form information. You can create a form document in any application that can print.

To create a form document:

1. Follow the steps outlined in Chapter 2 to create a PDF file. For this example, I've created a QuarkXPress file in a manner very similar to the way I would create a paper-based form. **Ⓐ**

2. Open the file in Acrobat Exchange 3.0. **Ⓑ**

At this point, the document is ready to have form fields added to it.

Ⓐ *The original document in QuarkXPress.*

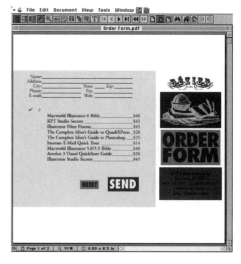

Ⓑ *The file converted to a PDF document and opened in Exchange.*

Form fields

Form fields are items designated for "user response." These items can be modified by anyone using Acrobat Reader 3.0. The items Acrobat allows user response on are:

• Buttons

• Check boxes

• Combo boxes

• List boxes

• Radio buttons

• Text fields

In addition, you can control various elements of each of these items, including their appearance and behavior. You can even control the tab order of text fields.

You can decide what URL (Uniform Resource Locator) the information is sent to. When the user "submits" the form information, it will be sent to that location automatically. URLs don't have to be just Web sites (www.site.com), they can also be FTP sites and even e-mail addresses!

Form fields are created primarily within Acrobat, although other Adobe applications such as PageMaker, FrameMaker, and Illustrator can specify form types or destinations before the file is turned into a PDF file.

All About Form Fields

To create a Form field in Acrobat Exchange:

1. Choose the Form tool from the Tools menu in Acrobat. **C**

2. Drag across the area you'd like to designate as a form. **D** For this example, I'm creating a text field form in the "Name" area of my PDF file.

When the mouse button is released, the Field Properties dialog box will be displayed, showing the Text Options tab. **E**

3. Change the properties (see next page) or click the OK button to use the default settings.

Field Properties Defaults

If you create a field without modifying the different options, the following default values will be in place:

A text field that is flush left, contains no "dummy" text, and exists only on one line, with no border or background color.

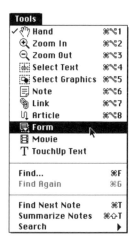

C *Choose the Form tool from the Tools menu.*

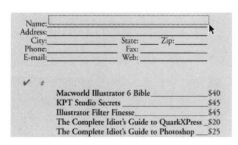

D *Drag with the Form tool to create a form block.*

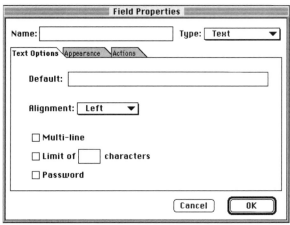

E *The Field Properties dialog box that appears when you create a form.*

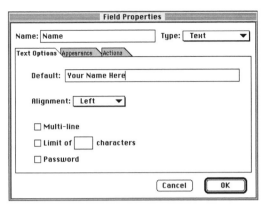

Field Properties

Name: Name   Type: Text ▼

Text Options Appearance Actions

Default: Your Name Here

Alignment: Left ▼

☐ Multi-line
☐ Limit of ⬚ characters
☐ Password

Cancel   OK

❶ *In the Default text field, enter any text that you would like to appear in that field before the user activates it.*

To change the Text Options in the Field Properties dialog box:

1. In the Field Properties dialog box, click on the Text Options tab. The Text Options will be displayed.

2. Enter the Name of the field. Since this field is the Name in my document, I've called the field "Name." Creative, eh?

3. In the Default text field, enter any text that you would like to have appear in the field before the user activates the text field. **❶** I've used "Your Name Here." For a similar Name field, you might use a pretend name like "Nancy Davis" or something like "Start Typing Here."

4. Choose the alignment of the text to be entered from the Alignment pop-up menu. I've left this option the default (left aligned).

5. Check the Multi-line box if you think the information being entered may take several lines of text. This would be a good option to choose if this field were to contain all the contact information, not just Name.

6. If you want to limit the number of characters that can be entered, check the box next to Limit of, and enter the number of characters to the left of the word "characters." This is useful if the software that will be reading the data is limited to a certain number of characters.

7. Check the Password box to make the text field work as a password reader (see Chapter 15).

Changing Text Options

To change the appearance in the Field Properties dialog box:

1. In the Field Properties dialog box, click on the Appearance tab. The Appearance options will be displayed. **G**

2. If you'd like the field to have a border, check the Border Color check box and change the color by clicking on the color to the right of the check box. I left this box unchecked in my example file, since I already drew underlines in QuarkXPress where the text would be placed.

3. If you'd like the field to have a background color that is different than the background of the file, check the Background Color box and choose a color by clicking on the icon to the right.

4. If you've chosen to place a border or a background color on the field, you can change the width and style of it by selecting a style from the Width and Style pop-up menus.

5. Change the font of the text that will be entered by selecting a font from the Font pop-up menu. You can also modify the color and size of the font in this area.

6. Click the OK button to put your changes into affect. **H**

7. Switch to the Hand tool to see how the field will look in Acrobat Reader. **I**

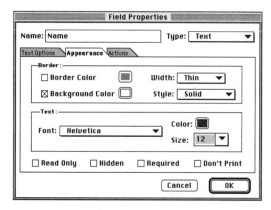

G *The Appearance tab in the Field Properties dialog box.*

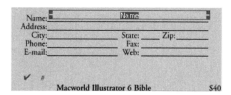

H *The field after being created, with the Form tool still selected.*

I *After changing to the Hand tool, the document appears as it will look in Acrobat Reader.*

Changing the Appearance of Fields

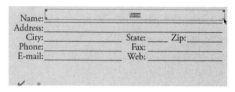

J *Click on the field with the Form tool to edit it.*

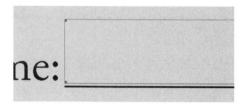

K *Zoom in while editing to make the field align with other objects.*

Name: [_____]
Address: [_____]
City: [_____] State: [____] Zip: [_____]
Phone: [_____] Fax: [_____]
E-mail: [_____] Web: [_____]

L *The final, resized and repositioned field.*

Name: Ted Alspach
Address: _____
City: _____
Phone: _____

M *Sample data entered into the adjusted field.*

To adjust a field's position and size:

1. Choose the Form tool from the Tools menu in Acrobat.

2. Click on the field you wish to modify. The handles of the field will appear, and the field will be surrounded by a red outline. **J**

3. Click on the center of the field and drag to move the field.

You can be more precise and accurate if you zoom in when you're adjusting. **K**

4. Click on the corner handles of the field to resize the field. **L**

5. After you're finished, check to make sure the field is the correct size by entering sample information into it. I used my name in this example. **M**

Adjusting the Size and Position of a Field

Instead of re-creating each field, you might find it easier to duplicate existing fields, especially if they'll be the same type of field and a similar size.

To duplicate an existing field:

1. Choose the Form tool from the Tools menu in Acrobat.

2. Press the Option key for Macintosh or the Alt key for Windows, click on the field you wish to duplicate, and drag to where you'd like the new field to be. **N**

3. Release the mouse button *before* releasing the Option/Alt key and the field will be duplicated.

4. Repeat this process until you've duplicated all the fields you need. **O**

5. Switch to the Hand tool to make sure the fields look correct. **P** You may need to change the sample text (which you can do with the Hand tool).

You can press the Shift key while dragging (or Option/Alt dragging) to constrain the movement of the dragged object to a 45° angle. This allows for more exacting placement than by freely dragging up/down or left/right.

ACROBAT 3 TIP

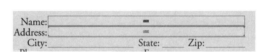

N *Option or Alt drag with the Form tool to create a duplicate of an existing field.*

Name:
Address:
City: State: Zip:
Phone: Fax:
E-mail: Web:

O *Option or Alt drag repeatedly until you've created enough duplicates.*

Name: Your Name Here
Address:
City: State: Zip:
Phone: Fax:
E-mail: Web:

P *Check the appearance of the duplicated fields by switching to the Hand tool.*

Duplicating Existing Fields

122

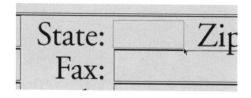

O *Draw the field with the Form Tool.*

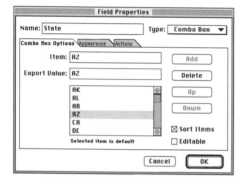

R *In the Field Properties dialog box, choose Combo Box as the Field Type.*

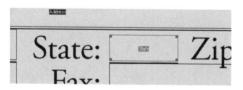

S *The field (with the Form tool selected) looks just like the other fields.*

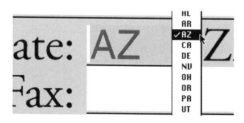

T *With the Hand tool selected, you can choose an item from the Combo Box field.*

A useful field type is the Combo Box field. This type of field lets the reader choose from several different options. The field can then be edited (or not, at your discretion). I used this field type for the State field.

To add a Combo Box field:

1. Choose the Form tool from the Tools menu in Acrobat.

2. Drag to draw the field on the page. **O**

3. In the Field Properties dialog box, choose Combo Box from the list of field types. **R**

4. Enter the first value you'd like the list to show when the viewer clicks on it. In this case the list shows several state abbreviations.

5. Enter the value you'd like to send for that choice. For instance, if you wanted the state information as numbers, you could enter a number for each state. In this way each state could send back a numeric value for computation within a spreadsheet, for instance.

6. Click the Add button. That item will be added to the list.

7. Repeat Steps 4 through 6 until all the items to be in the list are added.

8. Press the OK button when finished.

The field will look just like other fields when the Form tool is active. **S** When you switch to the Hand tool, you'll be able to choose an item from the Combo Box field pop-up menu. **T**

Adding a Combo Box Field

To create a Check Box field:

1. Choose the Form tool from the Tools menu in Acrobat.

2. Drag to draw the field on the page.

U *Draw the field with the Form Tool.*

3. In the Field Properties dialog box, choose "Check Box" from the list of field types. The leftmost tab will change to Check Box Options. **V**

4. Name the field.

5. Choose a check style (see following page) from the Check Style pop-up menu.

6. Enter what you'd like the Export Value to be. This is the value that will be returned (next to the style name) when the box is checked. "On" is the default value, but you might find a term such as "yes" or "good" is more appropriate for your form.

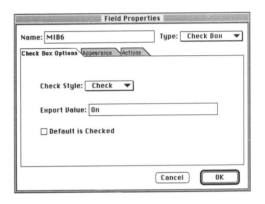

V *The Check Box Options.*

7. If you'd like the field to be checked by default, check the Default is Checked check box.

8. Click the OK button.

9. Change to the Hand tool to display the check box. **W** Click the box to see how it appears when checked. **X**

W *After selecting the Hand tool, the check box is shown unchecked.*

X *After selecting the Hand tool, click on the check box to see how it appears when checked.*

○ *The pop-up menu that shows the different Check Box styles.*

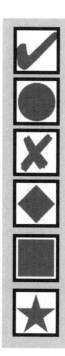

❷ *The different Check Box styles, from top to bottom: Check, Circle, Cross, Diamond, Square, and Star.*

There are several different styles of check boxes to select from in the Check Box Options window. In addition to changing the style of the check box, you can also change the color of the check and the border.

To change Check Box styles:

1. With the Form tool, double-click on the field you wish to change.

2. Select a different style from the ones listed in the Style pop-up menu. ○

The different styles are shown to the left. ❷

To change Check Box colors:

1. With the Form tool, double-click on the field you wish to change.

2. Click on the Appearance tab in the Field Properties dialog box. ⓐ

3. Choose a new Border Color and Background Color. The border color is the color that "frames" the check box. The background color is the color inside the check box.

4. Choose a different Text color. This color is actually the color of the "check."

5. Click the OK button.

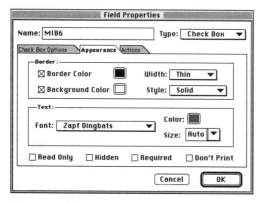

ⓐ *The Appearance tab of the Check Box options field type.*

The Check Box Styles

According to proper interface design, you should never use one radio button by itself. Therefore, the following steps show how to create one "set" of three radio buttons that work together.

To create each Radio Button:

1. Choose the Form tool from the Tools menu in Acrobat.

2. Drag to draw a field on the page.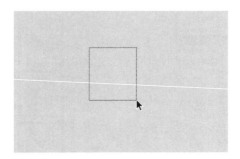

3. In the Field Properties dialog box, choose "Radio Button" from the list of field types. ⒸⒸ

4. Name the field and click the OK button.

5. Repeat steps 2 through 4 until there are three buttons on the page. ⒹⒹ

6. Select the Hand tool from the Tools menu to see the fields display as radio buttons. ⒺⒺ

ⒷⒷ *Drag to create a field with the Form tool.*

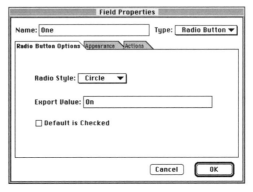

ⒸⒸ *The Radio Button Options screen.*

ⒺⒺ *The same three fields shown with the Hand tool selected.*

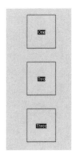

ⒹⒹ *Three fields shown with the Form tool selected.*

Using Radio Buttons

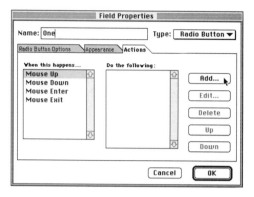

ⒻⒻ *The Actions tab of the Field Properties dialog box.*

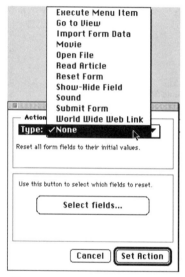

ⒼⒼ *The Actions palette, showing the Type pop-up menu.*

ⒽⒽ *The Field Selection dialog box.*

To link three Radio Buttons together:

1. With the Form tool, double-click on the first radio button.

2. Click on the Actions tab in the Field Properties dialog box. **ⒻⒻ**

3. Click the Add button.

4. In the Actions palette that appears, select Reset Form from the Type pop-up menu. **ⒼⒼ**

5. Click the Select fields button in the Actions palette.

6. In the Field Selection dialog box, click the Select fields button. **ⒽⒽ**

7. Select the other radio buttons, one at a time, and click the Include button. **ⅡⅡ**

8. Exit all the dialog boxes by clicking the highlighted button in each of them (OK, OK, Set Action, OK).

9. Repeat steps 1 through 8 with the other two radio buttons.

The buttons are now linked together.

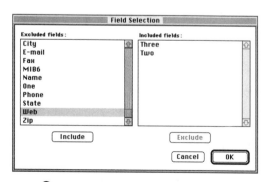

ⅡⅡ *Select each field and click Include to reset those fields when the current field is clicked.*

Linking Radio Buttons

Have you ever noticed that some functions and activities seem almost like second nature when you're choosing options within a dialog box? That's because there are certain rules that are followed in interface design. The most basic rules are those that define how certain types of objects act, and interact, with each other.

How Check Boxes work

Check boxes work in sets. **JJ** Within a set of check boxes, one, none, all, or any combination may be checked ("on"). Check boxes are very flexible and independent; checking any check box usually has no affect on any other check box within that set.

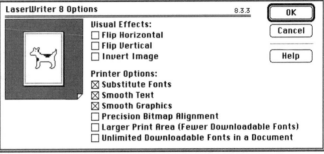

JJ *Check boxes are used to great effect in the Macintosh LaserWriter Page Setup dialog box.*

How Radio Buttons work

Radio buttons also come in sets. **KK** Within a set of radio buttons, only one (and always one) of those radio buttons will be active ("on"). In that way, radio buttons are like lists or Combo Boxes.

How Combo Boxes work

Combo Boxes are pop-up menus with editable text fields attached to them. The pop-up menu provides access to frequently-used or common options, inserting the chosen option in the text field automatically. If the viewer wants to enter a totally different setting, they can do so in the text field.

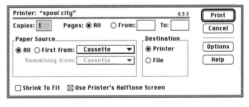

KK *The Print dialog box uses a variety of Radio Buttons.*

The overused catchword of the early 90s was indeed multimedia. Of course, a few years ago you needed a doctorate in Director in order to create anything remotely akin to multimedia.

Now, however, Acrobat provides a simple way for you to add buttons, movies, sounds, and other "multimedia-ish" components to PDF files. This means that you can create multimedia files in any program, from QuarkXPress (with no need for that hideous monstrosity "Immedia") to Adobe PageMaker, to Adobe Illustrator.

About Multimedia

TM

To set up a PDF document for Multimedia:

1. Create the "background" of the screen in any software that can create PDF Files. I used a background from Adobe Illustrator for the title screen of this production.

2. Create a PDF file from the background.

3. Open the background screen document in Acrobat Exchange. **Ⓐ**

4. If necessary, crop any excess portion of the page that appears around the edge of the screen background area using the Crop command. **Ⓑ**

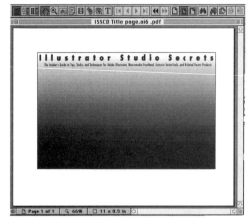

Ⓐ *The document when first opened in Acrobat Exchange.*

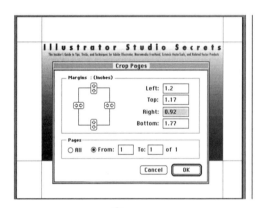

Ⓑ *The Crop Pages dialog box.*

Ⓒ *The document after it has been cropped.*

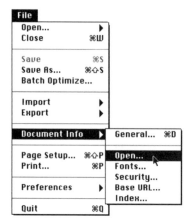

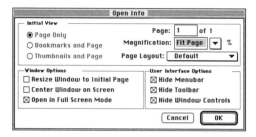

❶ *Choose Open from the Document Info submenu in the File menu.*

❷ *The Open Info dialog box, set up for "take control" mode.*

Many multimedia presentations are totally submersive; buttons, menus, and controls within the presentation control all facets. Many times, the presentation prevents the viewer from accessing standard menus and commands.

To have your document "take control" of the screen:

1. Choose Open from the Document Info submenu in the File menu. **❶** The Open Info dialog box will appear. **❷**

2. In the Window Options area, check Open in Full Screen Mode.

3. In the User Interface Options area, select all three options: Hide Menubar, Hide Toolbar, and Hide Window Controls.

The next time the document is opened in Exchange or Reader, the new options will go into effect.

Considerations when hiding standard interface components

Because the people reading your document will be lacking several things they're used to, such as the menu bar and toolbar, you may want to provide options to compensate for some of the capabilities you're hiding.

For instance, a multi-page document will need navigation buttons so viewers can go to the next and previous pages. A quit or exit button can be useful. If you have a main menu, or table of contents, you might want to make a button on each page that takes you there as well.

Taking Control of the Screen

131

Any element can be used as a button. One setting of Acrobat's Link tool allows for just that.

To turn an existing element into a button:

1. Choose the Link tool from the Tools menu. **F**

2. Drag the Link tool cursor around the object you wish to use as a button. When you release the mouse button, the Create Link palette will appear. **G**

3. Choose Invisible Rectangle from the Type pop-up menu.

4. Choose Inset from the Highlight pop-up menu.

5. Choose the type of action you'd like the button to perform from the Type pop-up menu in the Action area. For this example, because I'm using the "Send" button, I've chosen the Submit Form action.

6. Click the Set Link button.

The new button will look no different than before, and only the edges will change when the button is clicked on (with the Hand tool). **H**

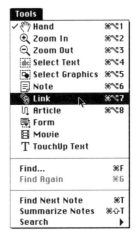

F *Choose Link from the Tools menu.*

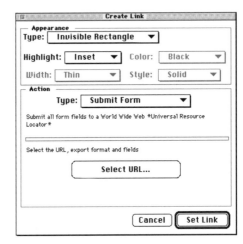

G *After drawing with the Link tool, the Create Link palette appears.*

H *The new "button" doesn't appear any different than before it was a button.*

Turning Elements into Buttons

Buttons can be created as separate PDF files to give a two-part appearance to button clicking. That is, the button will look one way until it is clicked, and then it will look different after it has been clicked.

To create two different button states:

1. Create the first button state (the way the button should look *before* it is pushed) in any software package.

For my example, I created a simple "go" button with bevels in Adobe Illustrator.

2. Create a PDF file out of the first button document.

3. Create the second button state (the way the button should look *after* it is pushed) in any software package.

The second button state should be the same size as the first button state, and contain similar artwork to the first button. For my example I added a starburst around the first button and changed the colors of the button.

4. Create a PDF file out of the second button document.

The first button (unpushed).

The second button (pushed).

Creating Before and After Button States

To add a PDF button to a PDF file:

1. In the multimedia document, choose the Form tool from the Tools menu.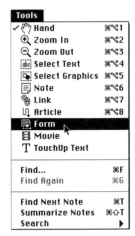

2. Drag to create the area in which the button will be placed. Try to approximate the dimensions of the button you've already created as a PDF file.

When you release the mouse button, the Field Properties dialog box will appear.

3. Select the button option from the Type pop-up menu. ❶ The Buttons Options screen will be displayed. ❶

4. In the Button Options screen, change the Highlight to Push.

5. Click the Icon button in the Appearance when UP area.

A standard open/save dialog box will appear.

6. Select the PDF file for the UP position of the button.

7. Click the Icon button in the Appearance when PUSHED area.

8. Select the PDF file for the PUSHED position of the button.

9. Click the OK button.

When you switch back to the Hand tool, the button will display in its up view. Clicking on the button will display its pushed view.

❶ *Choose the Form tool from the Tools menu.*

❶ *Choose Button from the Type pop-up menu at the top of the Field Properties dialog box.*

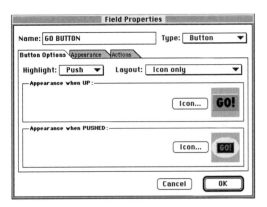

❶ *The Button Options screen with two different icons showing.*

Adding PDF Buttons

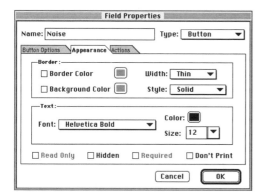

❶ *The Appearance tab of the Field Properties dialog box.*

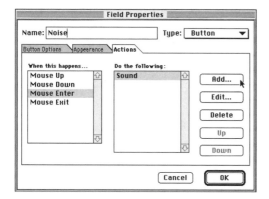

❷ *The Actions tab of the Field Properties dialog box.*

Acrobat doesn't require viewers to click on something in order to get feedback. Instead, you can set up Acrobat documents so that when the cursor passes over an area, some action happens. In this example, we're creating a sound pop-up menu.

To create a non-clicking interactive area:

1. Choose the Form tool from the Tools menu.

2. Drag to create the area you want to make non-clicking interactive.

3. In the Field Properties dialog box, choose Button from the Type pop-up menu.

4. Click on the Appearance tab. **❶** In the Appearance section, uncheck the Border Color and Background Color boxes.

5. Click on the Actions tab. **❷** Choose the Mouse Enter option in the When this happens list.

6. Click on the Add button. The Actions palette will appear.

7. Choose Sound from the Type list.

8. Click the Choose Sound button and select a sound file (Acrobat can read AIFF or System 7 sounds).

9. Click OK to exit the Action palette, and click OK to exit the Field Properties box.

Now, when you pass over the non-clicking interactive area with the Hand tool, the sound you've chosen will play.

Interactivity Without Clicking

Documents can be set up so that when a certain page is viewed, a certain activity happens. In this example a movie is played automatically when a page is viewed.

To create a movie that plays automatically:

1. Choose the Movie tool from the Tools menu.

2. Click and drag to set the size of the movie.

When you release the mouse button, the Open dialog box will appear.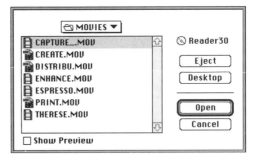

3. Choose a movie from the dialog box and click Open.

The Movie Properties dialog box will appear. ●

4. Click OK after you've made any changes to the Movie Properties dialog box.

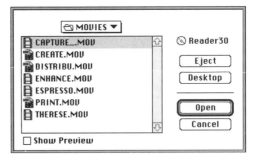

● *Select a movie to be displayed in the PDF document.*

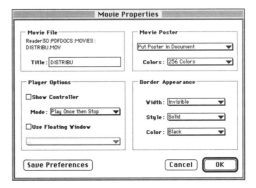

● *The Movie Properties dialog box.*

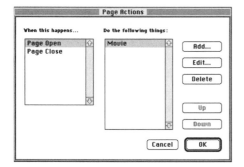

R *Choose Set Page Action from the Document menu.*

S *The Page Actions dialog box.*

5. Choose Set Page Action from the Document menu. **R**

6. In the Page Actions dialog box, click the Page Open item in the When this happens list. **S**

7. Click the Add button.

The Add Action palette will appear.

8. Select Play Movie from the Action Type menu and click OK.

9. Click OK in the Page Actions dialog box.

Now when the current page is displayed, the movie will play automatically.

Making a Movie Play Automatically

137

Wouldn't it be nice to automatically convert all your paper-based documents into PDF format? Those documents could then be archived electronically and distributed via e-mail or CD-ROM. Acrobat 3 provides a plug-in to do just that.

Acrobat Capture lets you scan in documents that contain images, text, multiple columns, and more, while retaining colors, fonts, and other elements.

In addition, you can convert already-scanned documents that are saved in various formats.

About Capture

All about Capture

Acrobat Capture is a stand-alone product designed to be used in conjunction with Acrobat. Acrobat 3.0 includes an Exchange plug-in that provides most of the features in the stand-alone product, but without Capture's Batch-scanning capabilities. Batch scanning allows you to scan multiple documents all at one time.

This chapter will focus on using the Capture Plug-in within Adobe Acrobat.

How Capture works

Capture looks at any scanned-in artwork and text on a page and converts the text into editable text within Acrobat. In addition, the art and text placement is maintained throughout the process of capturing.

Pages are imported into Acrobat (using either the Import->Image command or Import->Twain Acquire) and are converted into PDF documents at that time. After they've become PDF documents, selecting Capture from the Document menu converts the document text into editable characters. The benefit of this conversion is that now the text (as characters) takes up drastically less space than a comparable scan of the same text. In addition, minor edits can be done to text within Exchange, or the text can be heavily edited within Adobe Illustrator.

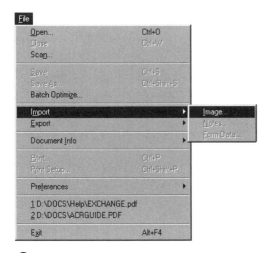

A *Choose Image from the Import submenu in the File menu.*

B *The Import image dialog box.*

To import an image to be captured:

1. Choose Image from the Import submenu of the File menu. **A**

The Import image dialog box will appear. **B**

2. Select the file to be imported. In this example, I'll import a file called "textblck."

Acrobat will convert the image into a PDF document.

To import a scan to be captured:

1. Choose Twain Acquire from the Import submenu of the File menu. This menu item only appears if you have a scanner installed on your computer that supports the standard Twain functions.

The scanning window for your scanner will appear.

2. Select the area of the page to be scanned and click OK (scanning software varies; your scanning screen may require different procedures).

Acrobat will convert the image into a PDF document.

Importing Images and Scans

Once the image is imported into Acrobat Exchange, it is ready to be "captured." This process turns text into editable characters, and images into stand-alone image objects within the document.

To capture an image:

1. Choose Capture Pages from the Document menu. **ⓒ**

The Acrobat Capture Plug-in dialog box will appear. **ⓓ**

2. Select Current Page and click the OK button.

If you have more than one page in your document, select either All Pages to capture each page or Specified Range to capture a certain range of page (i.e., pages 4–8).

3. Click the OK button.

Various dialog boxes will appear, indicating the progress of the conversion. When the conversion is finished, the document will appear in captured form.

The facing page shows the PDF document prior to being captured **ⓔ** and after being captured. **ⓕ**

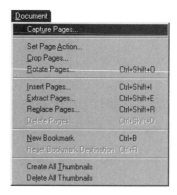

ⓒ *Choose Capture Pages from the Document menu.*

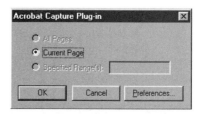

ⓓ *Choose which pages of the current PDF document to capture in this dialog box.*

Capturing Images

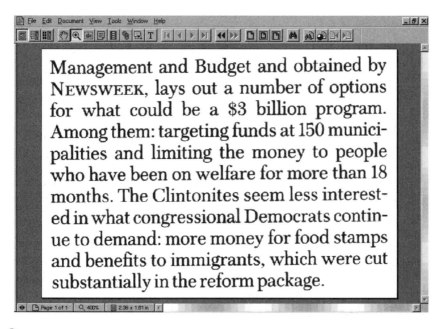

❶ *The original PDF image, showing the scanned letters. Note that this image is slightly crooked.*

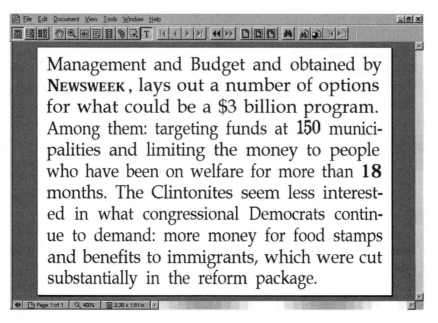

❶ *The same PDF document after being captured. The text is straightened automatically.*

Before and After Capturing

To edit captured text:

1. Choose the Text tool from the Tools menu.

2. Click on the text you'd like to edit.

Because the text is now in editable character form, you can change letters, spelling, and punctuation by selecting the letter to be changed and typing the new letter.

3. Double-click to select a word; drag after double-clicking to select a word at a time. **H** Click and drag to select individual characters or portions of words.

4. Type in the replacement character(s).

5. Switch back to the Hand tool by choosing it from the Tools menu.

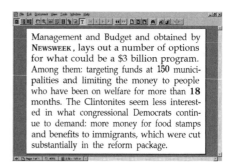

G *The PDF document after being captured is now ready for minor text edits.*

Management and Budget and obtained by NEWSWEEK, lays out a number of options for what could be a $3 billion program.

H *The word "Management" has been selected with the Text tool.*

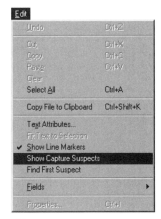

❶ *Choose Show Capture Suspects from the File menu.*

❶ *The Capture Suspect dialog box shows what Acrobat thinks should go in place of the bitmapped image area in question.*

Occasionally, Acrobat's Capture plug-in will have trouble interpreting a word or character. When that happens, Acrobat substitutes what it thinks is probably correct, and marks the word or character as "suspect."

You can review the suspects within a captured PDF by following the steps outlined below.

To find and review suspects:

1. Choose Show Capture Suspects from the File menu. ❶

The Capture Suspect dialog box will appear, showing the first "suspect" occurrence. ❶

2. Press the Tab key to accept Acrobat's interpretation or click the Next button to find the next suspect. Pressing the Tab key will not only accept the interpretation, but will also move to the next suspect automatically. If you don't accept the suspect, you can leave the bitmapped image in place.

3. Repeat step 2 until you've reviewed all the suspect areas.

Are you concerned that your document may fall into the wrong hands? Or maybe you'd like to distribute your document electronically, but don't want that document printed and possibly distributed to unauthorized users.

Acrobat's built-in security options can prevent unauthorized access, printing, and editing of your PDF files. Secured PDF files will stand up to rigorous attempts to bypass their password-protection schemes.

Security Concerns

TM

To prevent unauthorized opening of a document:

1. Open the document you wish to protect in Acrobat Exchange.

2. Choose Save As from the File menu. **Ⓐ**

The Save As dialog box will appear.

3. Click the Security button. **Ⓑ**

The Security Options dialog box appears.

4. Enter a password in the Open the Document text field. **Ⓒ**

5. Click the OK button.

The Confirm Password dialog box appears. **Ⓓ**

6. Type in the password again, and click OK.

7. Click the Save button.

At this point the document is protected. If you close the document now, the only way it can be reopened is by supplying the correct password.

Ⓐ *Choose Save As from the File menu.*

Ⓑ *Click the Security button in the Save As dialog box.*

Ⓓ *Confirm your password by retyping it in this dialog box.*

Ⓒ *Enter a password in the Open the Document text field.*

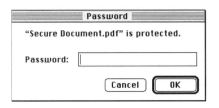

❺ *Enter the password in order to open the password-protected document.*

❻ *If you enter the wrong password, click the OK button to try again. If you enter the wrong password three times, you'll have to reopen the document.*

To open a locked PDF file:

1. Double-click on the file, or select it from the Open dialog box within Acrobat.

The Password dialog box appears, notifying you that the document you are trying to open is protected by a password. **❺**

2. Enter the password and click the OK button to open the document.

If you enter the correct password, the document will open.

If you enter the wrong password, the Incorrect password box will appear. **❻**

3. If you encountered the Incorrect password dialog box, click the OK button.

4. Enter the correct password and click the OK button.

After a wrong password has been entered three times, the dialog box ceases to appear, and the document must be opened again by double-clicking its icon or using the Open dialog box of Acrobat.

Opening Locked PDF Files

> You can easily change the Open Document password of a locked PDF document. Open the document, choose Save As, and type a new password in the Security window. If you don't enter a password there, the password protection will be removed entirely.
>
> **ACROBAT 3 TIP**

Besides the ability to prevent a document from being opened without a password, Acrobat provides several other levels of protection.

Other security options

In the Security Options dialog box (access by clicking the Security button in the Save As dialog box), there are four other options that can be controlled: **G**

Printing. This option prevents the printing of the PDF document. The Print command in the File menu is grayed out (and Command-P for Macintosh and Control+P for Windows are disabled).

Changing the Document. This option prevents pages from being added or removed, and document options from being changed. It also prevents security options from being modified. In addition, the Document menu is grayed out. **H**

Selecting Text and Graphics. Checking this option prevents text and graphics from being selected. This can prevent text and graphics from being copied and pasted.

Adding or Changing Notes and Form Fields. This option prevents Notes and Form Fields from being changed. Don't check this option in a document that contains form fields you want readers to fill out.

G *The additional options in the Do Not Allow area of the Security Options dialog box.*

H *The Document menu with all the security options grayed out.*

How to choose a password

If keeping your document secure is important, then the most important thing you can do is to have a good password. When choosing a password, keep the following rules in mind:

Don't Write it Down Anywhere. If you can't remember it, don't use it. Writing down a password is just like duplicating a key and leaving it laying around. If you have to write it down, use some type of encoding that only you will understand, maybe something like every third character.

Don't pick an Easy Guesser. What's an Easy Guesser? The name of a friend, pet, or spouse. Your social security number. A date, especially your birthday.

Combine Numerals and Letters. If you use only numbers in an eight-character password, there are ten million combinations. Sounds like a lot, but a professional experienced with password decryption can zip through them quicker than you'd believe. If you use a combination of eight letters and numbers, the combinations total almost three trillion.

Make Your Password Easy to Remember, but Hard to Guess. If someone you know can guess your password before someone you *don't* know could guess it, your password is too easy to guess. If you have to write it down, it's too hard to remember.

Choosing a Password

The World Wide Web has transformed the entire world into an ugly HTML-based society of patiently waiting-for-connection Internet junkies. It wouldn't be too bad if HTML was compact, flexible, and produced good-looking content, but as we all know, that's certainly not the case.

Adobe was late in anticipating the popularity of the Web, as were Microsoft and a host of other companies. However, instead of shoring up to fight the browser wars, Adobe decided to go another route: to take its existing PDF technology and optimize it for the Web.

This chapter discusses how to use Acrobat and PDF files on the Web, from creating and displaying pages on your Web server, to reading them online.

Why Adobe Doesn't Have an HTML Browser

TM

Acrobat 3.0 files can be viewed live on the Internet by Netscape and Internet Explorer Web browsers. The pages are sent one at a time, so if a reader wants to view just pages 1, 3, 16 and 243, they don't get the entire 300 page document downloaded.

Only PDF documents provided in 3.0 format can be downloaded one page at a time; 2.1 and older PDF files are downloaded in their entirety to the requesting Web browser.

To set up your Web browser to read PDF files:

1. Open your Adobe Acrobat 3.0 folder/directory. A window will appear showing its contents. **Ⓐ**

2. Open the Web Browser Plug-in folder/directory. A window will appear that contains the PDFViewer icon. **Ⓑ**

3. Open your browser's folder/directory. A window will appear showing its contents.

4. Drag the PDFViewer plug-in into the browser's Plug-Ins folder/directory. **Ⓒ**

The next time you run your Web browser, you'll be able to read PDF files with it.

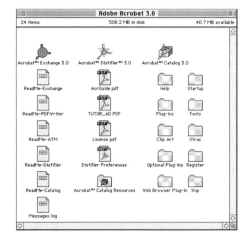

Ⓐ *The Adobe Acrobat 3.0 window. The Web Browser Plug-in folder is in the lower right corner.*

Ⓑ *The Web Browser Plug-in window. The only item in this window is the PDFViewer plug-in icon.*

Ⓒ *Drag the PDFViewer icon into the Plug-ins folder of your Web browser.*

Choose Open Location from the File menu of your Web browser.

Enter the URL in the text field.

The sample page when loaded.

To view a test PDF document within your browser:

1. Launch your Web browser and confirm that you're on the Web.

2. Choose Open Location from the File menu. **D**

The Open Location dialog box appears. **E**

3. Enter the following into the text field, then click the OK button:

```
http://www.bezier.com/
AVQSPDF.PDF
```

The PDF plug-in will load, and then the page will be displayed. **F**

Acrobat Reader (or Exchange, if it is on your system) will load as an application in the background, so you'll need enough free RAM to support both your browser and the Acrobat application to run at the same time.

To view any PDF documents within your browser:

1. Launch your Web browser and confirm that you're on the Web.

2. Click on any link that is a PDF file.

Most PDF file links will have the .PDF extension after them.

Viewing PDF Files on the Web

While Acrobat 3.0 files can be read online one page at a time, not all Acrobat 3.0 files can be read this way. Some Acrobat 3.0 files will download the entire file before displaying the first page of the document. For Acrobat PDF 3.0 files to be read one page at a time, they need to be optimized.

The process of displaying one page at a time is called *byteserving*. In order to make byteserving work, the PDF files need to be optimized at the time of saving.

To optimize PDF files for byte-serving:

1. With the PDF file open, choose Save As from the File menu.

2. Check the Optimize check box in the Save As dialog box.

3. Click the Save button.

The file is now ready to be placed on a Web server for downloading.

G *Choose Save As from the File menu.*

H *Check the Optimize check box in the Save As dialog box.*

If you make changes to your PDF file after you have done a Save As to optimize it, do *not* merely Save the file when you've finished making your changes. Instead, do another Save As. If you don't Save As, the optimization is removed.

ACROBAT 3 TIP

Choose Batch Optimize from the File menu.

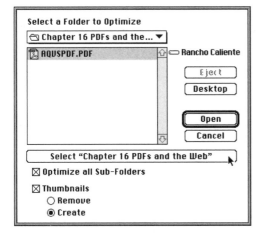

Select the folder which contains the PDFs to be optimized.

If you have to optimize several PDF files, opening each and doing a Save As can be overly time consuming. Also, if you think you may have forgotten to optimize one PDF out of a hundred, there's no way to check, except by testing each PDF document individually.

To make tasks like this simpler, and to batch-convert PDFs created with version 2.1 (or older) into optimized 3.0 files, a batch converting utility is part of Acrobat Exchange.

To batch optimize several PDF files:

1. Within Acrobat Exchange, choose Batch Optimize from the File menu.

   The Select a Folder to Optimize dialog box will appear.

2. Locate the folder you wish to optimize.

3. If you want to optimize all the PDFs within sub-folders/sub-directories, check the Optimize all Sub-Folders check box.

4. If you want to Add or Remove Thumbnails to your documents, check the Thumbnails checkbox and choose the appropriate option.

   Thumbnails can substantially increase the size of PDFs.

5. Click the Select "Your Folder" button.

   The optimization process will begin. The Batch Operation Progress box will be displayed while Acrobat is optimizing.

The progress bar shows the current status of optimization.

Batch Optimizing PDF Files

157

Your Web administrator can probably tell you if your Web site is already set up to byteserve PDF files. If it is not set up this way, the Web site will need to have a CGI script installed.

Your Web administrator will know how to install this script, but you may need to supply the script for him or her.

To find a CGI script to allow byteserving of PDF files:

In your Web browser, go to Adobe's Web site which contains server scripts:

    http://www.adobe.com/prodindex/
    acrobat/webserve.html

This Web site 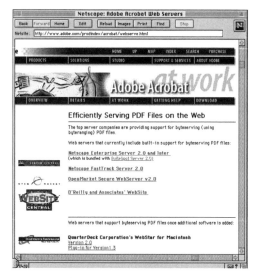 contains all the current server scripts for a variety of Web server software. It also contains a generic DOS/UNIX script that may work with other software.

In addition, it lists the current server software that has PDF byteserving built in.

Currently, the server software that supports PDF byteserving is:

Netscape Enterprise Server 2.0

Netscape FastTrack Server 2.0

OpenMarket Secure WebServer 2.0

WebStar 2.0 (for Macintosh).

Check with your internet service provider to ensure that they use either one of the packages listed above or that they can install a server script on your Web server.

Adobe's Web page listing scripts and compatible server software.

Byteserving PDF Files

File

Open...	⌘O
Close	⌘W
Save	⌘S
Save As...	⌘⇧S
Batch Optimize...	
Import	▶
Export	▶
Document Info	▶
Page Setup...	⌘⇧P
Print...	⌘P
Preferences	▶
Quit	⌘Q

ⓜ *Choose Save As from the File menu.*

ⓝ *Uncheck the Optimize button in the Save As dialog box.*

You can force viewers to download an entire document at once instead of page by page. If they have an entire document on their system, they'll be able to access individual pages much faster than if they had to be downloaded individually. Of course, all the time for downloading will be there, it'll just be taken care of in one long download. To do this, you must create non-optimized files.

To remove the optimization of PDF files to prevent byteserving:

1. With the PDF file open, choose Save As from the File menu. **ⓜ**

2. Uncheck the Optimize checkbox in the Save As dialog box. **ⓝ**

3. Click the Save button.

The file will now be downloaded in its entirety when viewed through or with a Web browser.

Providing Non-Optimized PDF Files

159

To seamlessly combine HTML and PDF documents is actually much easier than you'd expect. Adobe has designed Acrobat 3 with HTML integration in mind.

HTML pages can be linked to PDF pages, which can be read directly within the HTML browser. PDF pages can be embedded within HTML pages, so the PDF document appears as its own image or as a frame within an HTML page.

While Adobe has done its part to make the transition from HTML to PDF as simple as possible, there are several things you can do when creating a Web site to help your viewers jump back and forth between the two formats as transparently as possible.

TM

To create an HTML link to a PDF document:

1. In your HTML editor, type the line:

```
<A HREF="MyFile.PDF">
```

where MyFile.PDF is the name of the PDF file to which you wish to create a link.

If MyFile.PDF is in a different directory than the current HTML file, you'll need to include that file directory path.

2. On the next line, type the words you want to use as the visible "link."

```
Click here to view my PDF
document
```

3. On the last line, type:

```
</A>
```

That tells the browser that the previous line should be underlined and indicated as a link when viewed. **Ⓐ**

When anyone viewing your HTML page clicks on that link, their browser will load the PDFViewer plug-in and the document will be displayed within their browser window.

If the viewing browser does not have the PDFViewer plug-in installed, the PDF file will be downloaded via FTP.

Click here to view my PDF document

Ⓐ *This is how the link to your PDF document would appear in a Web browser such as Netscape Navigator.*

Some of the people visiting your web site may not have Acrobat Reader 3 installed on their systems. Because of this, you may want to post a notice on your home page, or any other page that has links to PDF documents, that Acrobat 3's PDFViewer plug-in is recommended for viewing that page.

To go one step further, you may want to include a link to Adobe's FTP site so that Acrobat Reader 3 can be downloaded immediately.

To create a link for downloading Acrobat Reader 3 for Macintosh:

1. In your HTML editor, type the line:

```
<A HREF="ftp://ftp.adobe.com/
pub/adobe/acrobatreader/mac/
2.x/ardr30e.bin">
```

2. On the next line, type the words you want to use as the visible "link."

```
Click here to download
Acrobat Reader for
Macintosh.
```

3. On the last line, type:

```
</A>
```

That tells the browser that the previous line should be underlined and indicated as a link when viewed.

Creating a Link for Macintosh Reader 3

To create a link for downloading Acrobat Reader 3 for Windows 95 or Windows NT:

1. In your HTML editor, type the line:

```
<A HREF="ftp://ftp.adobe.com/
pub/adobe/acrobatreader/
win/3.x/ar32e30.exe">
```

2. On the next line, type the words you want to use as the visible "link."

```
Click here to download
Acrobat Reader for Windows
95.
```

3. On the last line, type:

```
</A>
```

To create a link for downloading Acrobat Reader 3 for Windows 3.1:

1. In your HTML editor, type the line:

```
<A HREF="ftp://ftp.adobe.com/
pub/adobe/acrobatreader/
win/3.x/ar16e30.exe">
```

2. On the next line, type the words you want to use as the visible "link."

```
Click here to download
Acrobat Reader for Windows
3.1.
```

3. On the last line, type:

```
</A>
```

Because not all of your Web site visitors will have the PDFViewer plug-in installed when they come across your Web site, there are a number of different ways to accommodate both the haves and have nots.

The best way to create a PDF-based Web site is to start with an HTML pre-home page that lets the viewer know that the primary content is PDF-based, and that they'll need PDFViewer to continue. On this page, you might also want to provide a link to a few other HTML pages on your site that contain a limited version of your site's pages.

To create a pre-home page:

1. Rename your PDF-based home page to something other than its original name (you might want to add a ".pdf" suffix).

2. Create a new HTML page.

3. In the new page, create a link to your old home page.

4. Also in the new page, create a link to another new, HTML-based page.

This new page will contain a summary of what is on the rest of your PDF-based Web site.

5. Save the new page, naming it as your original home page.

Home Page Techniques

Individual PDF pages can be embedded within HTML pages just like JPEG or GIF images.

To embed a PDF page within an HTML page:

1. Where you'd like to embed the PDF page, type the following line:

```
<IMG SRC="MyPage.PDF">
```

2. If you'd like to make the PDF document appear at 50% of the original, type:

```
<IMG SRC="MyPage.PDF"
Height=50%>
```

If you enter a different percentage, the document will be scaled to that size.

To view an embedded PDF page:

1. View the HTML page that contains the PDF page. The PDF page will show up at the size you specified.

2. Click on the embedded PDF page.

The PDF page will open in Acrobat Reader automatically at the size specified within the PDF file.

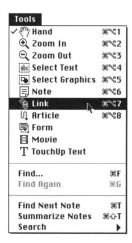

B *Choose Link from the Tools menu.*

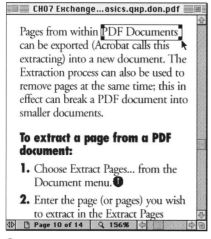

C *Drag around the area that will make up the link.*

To create a link from one spot in a PDF document to a URL on the Web:

1. Choose Link from the Tools menu. **B**

2. Drag around the area you wish to define as a link. **C**

   When you release the mouse button, the Link Properties palette will appear.

3. Choose World Wide Web Link from the Type pop-up menu.

4. Click the Edit URL button. The URL Edit dialog box will appear. **D**

5. Enter the URL that you'd like the link to go to, and click the OK button.

   When that link is clicked, your Web browser will start up and attempt to connect to that site.

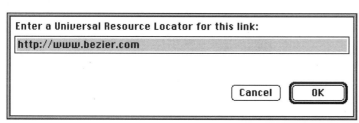

D *The URL Edit dialog box.*

Creating PDF Links to HTML Pages

You may not consider fonts to be all that relevant to PDF documents, but they're an intrinsic part of how PDFs work.

The decision of whether and how to include fonts is critical. It affects both the size and appearance of the document.

Acrobat automatically installs Adobe Type Manager (ATM) and special "substitution fonts" during the Acrobat 3 installation process. It is this utility and these fonts which enable you to choose *not* to include fonts, and still allow the document to look pretty much like the original document with the correct fonts.

In addition to this issue, there are many other font considerations to keep in mind when designing documents that will eventually end up in PDF form.

TM

Embedding fonts

Whenever you create a PDF document, you'll always have the option of embedding fonts into that document. Whether you do (or not) depends on several different criteria.

I've found that I choose to embed fonts more than 90 percent of the time, only choosing not to embed when I'm desperately trying to keep file sizes to a minimum. Not that fonts really add that much overhead, but 10K here and there can quickly add up to several megabytes.

When to embed

Always choose to embed fonts (via the Distiller or PDF Writer options) in the following situations:

- When the document is being used for proofing (appearance, not text)

- When the document contains text such as part of a logo that *must* be a certain font.

- When the fonts are decorative, graphical, or symbol-based (such as Zapf Dingbats or Carta).

- When the document needs to be used as a substitute for the original document.

- When the document is being sent to a service bureau or other place for final output.

The images to the right show the difference between a PDF with embedded fonts **A** and without embedded fonts. **B**

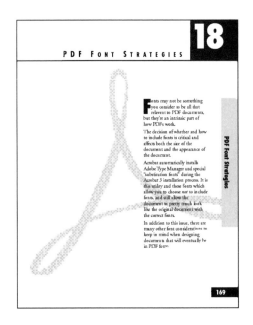

A *A PDF of the first page of this chapter shown with fonts embedded.*

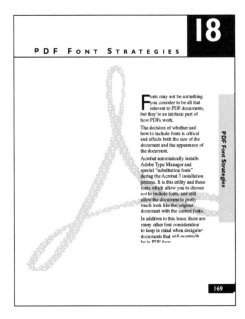

B *A PDF of the first page of this chapter shown with fonts* not *embedded.*

ACROBAT 3 TIP

Anti-aliasing is the process used for on-screen graphics and fonts to make them look smoother. This is accomplished by making pixels along curved and diagonal edges of characters a blend of the character color (usually black) and the background color (usually white).

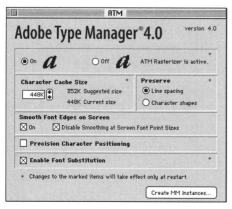

☉ *The ATM 4.0 control panel.*

Should fonts be anti-aliased?

It seems like a pretty straightforward question, but the issue of on screen anti-aliasing is one that is sure to plague most users of Acrobat Reader.

Acrobat Reader installs ATM version 4.0**☉**, which includes the ability to anti-alias fonts. The thing is, this doesn't work for only Acrobat Reader, but also for *every application on your computer.*

Personally, I like the way fonts look when they're anti-aliased on screen. However, I typically use a great big 20" monitor and zoom my pages in QuarkXPress, PageMaker and Illustrator to at least 150%. Even standard size fonts (10 and 12 point) look pretty good when they're 15 and 18 points large in anti-aliased view. But whenever I zoom out, I have trouble reading small anti-aliased type.

Fortunately, ATM 4.0 allows you to turn off anti-aliasing at screen font sizes. Most fonts have pre-built screen fonts at 12 points, so at this size or smaller, the fonts will not be anti-aliased.

To turn off anti-aliasing for screen font sizes:

1. Display the ATM Control Panel. Select Control Panels from the Apple menu (Macintosh) or Start menu (Windows), and double-click on ATM.

2. Check the "Disable Smoothing at Screen Font Point Sizes" checkbox.

3. Close the ATM window.

Anti-aliasing Fonts

Making sure the text size is appropriate for the column width (and vice versa)

This particular issue can be a thorny one, especially since readers can't alter the column widths and font sizes of PDFs you send them.

Acrobat Reader has three useful viewing modes: Fit Page 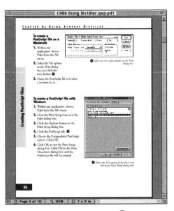, in which the entire page is sized to fit within the Reader window; Fit Width 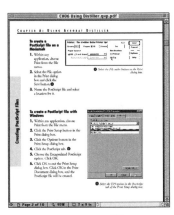, in which the page is sized so that the width of the page fits snugly in the Reader window; and Fit Visible 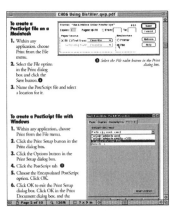, in which only the visible portions of the page are fit into the width of the Reader window.

Fit Page view.

All of these modes change the size of the page, but the readability of the text on the page depends on how much type there is per line. Generally, the less type per line, the more readable the text is. (Along those lines, I've made the columns in this book as narrow as possible.) The trick is to hold the reader's attention and focus from one line to the next. If lines are too long, the reader may skip a line or read a line twice, causing him or her to pause and have to reread the lines in order to make sense of the text.

Fit Width view.

In addition, if you've set up articles in your document, a reader viewing those articles will see them expand to the full width of the Reader window; if the lines of text contain too many characters, it's quite easy to become disoriented.

Fit Visible view.

Making PDF documents more readable by choosing the correct typeface

Type on a computer screen looks different than printed type. In order to provide the best viewing experience for readers of your PDF documents, you should constrain the use of typefaces to only those that look good on screen.

You can tell pretty easily what looks good on screen just by typing a few sentences and selecting different fonts right on your computer.

Things to avoid when choosing fonts for online viewing:

- Big serifs. Fonts like Tiffany, which have lovely large serifs, look great when printed but terrible on a monitor; sometimes the serifs begin to resemble other characters.

- Fonts with drastically varying stroke weights. Bodoni is a classic example of such a font; the vertical strokes are nice and thick, while the horizontal strokes are thin as can be, making them difficult to read on screen.

- Massively thick fonts. If the "holes" in fonts are difficult to see on screen, they can reduce readability.

Also, try to avoid excessive tracking or kerning, and don't horizontally scale type less than 70%.

Readability of Fonts On Screen

In print publishing, enormous graphics files are the norm rather than the exception. It's all too common to provide a service bureau with a Zip cartridge so a weekly newsletter can be printed. The size of the files involved is of secondary concern to appearance, with placed images often exceeding 10Mb a piece.

However, when publishing PDF documents, size is a much larger issue. In fact, the difference between waiting just a few seconds and several minutes for something to print is measured in Kilobytes, not Megabytes. The way graphics are initially inserted and saved can dramatically change the size of a PDF document. Further, the type of graphics used can also affect the size of that document.

PDF Graphics Strategies

JPEG compression

JPEG (Joint Photographic Experts Group) compression is one of the two standards of image compression, and currently the one with the most options.

Images that are compressed in JPEG format retain most of the colors (within a range of millions) in the original image, while losing a moderate amount of detail. So little detail is lost that most people outside the graphics industry can't tell the difference between the original and the modified JPEG image.

JPEG is a "lossy" form of compression, meaning that each time an image is saved as a JPEG, more of the original information is lost. Fortunately, you can have some degree of control over the amount of the image loss by choosing from various options when saving: from a limited amount of compression (and thus more original detail is maintained) to much greater amounts of compression (and less detail). Using the maximum amount of JPEG compression can reduce a file to 5% of its original size, or even less.

To set Acrobat Distiller to JPEG compression:

1. Choose Job Options from the Distiller menu. **A**

2. Click on the Compression tab in the Job Options dialog box. **B**

3. Change the first two Automatic Compression pop-up menus to ZIP/JPEG High.

4. Click the OK button.

A *Choose Job Options from the Distiller menu.*

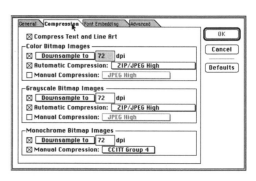

B *Click on the Compression tab to view the different graphics compression options.*

GIF compression

The GIF (Graphics Interchange Format) was developed by CompuServe more than ten years ago to help keep the size of online files small. The current incarnation of GIF is GIF89A, which includes the ability to have transparent areas (which can be set in any software that creates GIF89A images).

The major limitation of the GIF format is that it restricts graphics to a set number of colors, never more than 256. When cross-platform documents are being created, there are really only 216 colors that can be used (that's the number of colors that are the same between both Macintosh and Windows platforms). However, it is this limitation that allows the GIF format to be rather flexible. Instead of losing image data as with JPEG, GIF images retain each pixel's "difference" in color, but the color itself is often changed in order to fall within the limitations of the number of colors used. For monochrome images or images with only a few colors, GIF is an excellent choice.

C *Choose Job Options from the Distiller menu.*

D *Click on the Compression tab to view the different graphics compression options. Uncheck the Automatic and Manual compression checkboxes.*

To set Acrobat Distiller to maintain GIF image formats:

1. Choose Job Options from the Distiller menu. **C**

2. Click on the Compression tab in the Job Options dialog box. **D**

3. Uncheck the Automatic and Manual compression checkboxes.

4. Click the OK button.

Using GIF Compression

Vector graphics

One of the biggest, usually undiscovered, strengths of the PDF file format is that it can contain and maintain vector graphics, such as those created with Adobe Illustrator. Vector Object information is saved entirely within a PDF document; this allows the vector graphics to be displayed at any zoom level, and still maintain "perfect" quality. Another advantage of vector graphics is that using them can take up less space than an equivalent bitmap image.

Unfortunately, the opposite is also true of detailed vector graphics, especially those with large amounts of type that have been converted into outlines. In fact, when creating vector graphics for placement in PDF files, it's almost never a good idea to change type to outlines (unless some special effect needs to be applied to the text which can only be done to outlined paths). The more detail in a vector graphic, the more space it will consume (on a disk).

However, this detail can be useful if the physical size of the graphic is limited to a small amount of square inches, because Acrobat Reader can zoom in to the artwork dramatically, increasing detail.

You can keep file size to a minimum by creating PDF files from software that doesn't require you to save Illustrator documents as EPS before placing them into page layout programs. Unfortunately, the only major product (besides Illustrator) that allows this is PageMaker (QuarkXPress requires you to save the illustrations in EPS form).

Smaller PDFs are better PDFs

When creating PDF documents, often the most important consideration is how to keep the size of the file as small as possible. There are a number of ways to do this, but the most effective are:

- Use as few fonts as possible. This includes limiting the use of bold and italic (and bold italic) variations of a font, as each variation is really a separate font.

- Limit the use of graphics in publications to only those that are necessary.

- Use the compression options in Acrobat Distiller's Job Options dialog box, such as downsampling and JPEG compression.

- Use the subset option within the Font Embedding section of Acrobat Distiller's Job Options dialog box.

- Use vector graphics for large, solid areas where possible.

Keeping the File Size Small

How Downsampling Works

Downsampling is the process of changing the resolution of any image from its placed size in a document to 72 dpi. This can dramatically decrease the size of a bitmap image, and it's an option that is enabled by default in Acrobat Distiller.

The drawback to downsampling is that when a document is viewed larger than 100%, the image will appear blocky and pixelated.

To turn off downsampling in Acrobat Distiller:

1. Choose Job Options from the Distiller menu.

2. Click on the Compression tab in the Job Options dialog box.

3. Uncheck the Downsample checkboxes. **G**

4. Click the OK button.

To turn on downsampling in Acrobat Distiller:

1. Choose Job Options from the Distiller menu.

2. Click on the Compression tab in the Job Options dialog box.

3. Check the Downsample checkboxes and enter the dpi for each image (usually 72 dpi). **G**

4. Click the OK button.

E *Choose Job Options from the Distiller menu.*

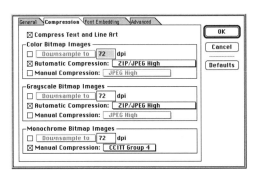

F *Click on the Compression tab and uncheck the Downsample checkboxes.*

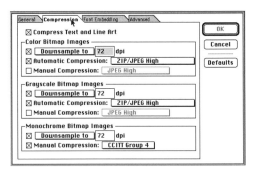

G *Click on the Compression tab, check the Downsample checkboxes, and enter the dpi for downsampling.*

Downsampling

White Space

If you've ever taken an art or design class, you've probably heard your instructor rant about white space and negative space and balance and many other things which you filed away as "typical bunk."

White space is the name given by designers to, er, white space on a page. The idea behind white space is that it's a relaxing area of a page. It takes the busy feel away from the page and creates a more inviting look that is supposed to draw you in. I've never been a big fan of white space, but I do agree that filling a page up with as much text and graphics as will fit is often counterproductive.

The great thing about using white space in PDF documents is that it costs practically nothing. So what if your PDF document is 12 or 20 pages long; if the same amount of text is used, the document will be almost the *exact same size*. Unlike the world of printing, where adding eight extra pages to a 12-page document would cost 67% more, adding empty space to PDF documents is "free."

Take advantage of this incredibly inexpensive space by being a little more creative with your page design. **H**

White Space is Your Friend

H *White space used in a document.*

Backgrounds and PDF Pages

Adding solid color backgrounds to PDF pages is extremely cheap in terms of file size. In programs like Adobe PageMaker and QuarkXPress, solid color backgrounds take up very little extra space.

Backgrounds with tiled patterns or large, faded graphics are a different matter, however. Stay away from complex backgrounds, as the files needed for these backgrounds can be absolutely huge.

The images to the right show three different backgrounds for this page. Only text and the common graphical elements (boxes, lines) were on the page; illustrations were excluded.

The image at the top has no background and is 33K. ❶

The second image has one solid color background and is 33K. ❶

The third image has several solid color backgrounds and is 33K. ❶

The fourth image uses a TIFF image as the background. With the standard Acrobat Distiller options on, the file size is 41K. ❶

❶ *Without a background, this PDF file is 33K (33,189 bytes) on disk.*

❶ *With a solid background, this PDF file is 33K (33,201 bytes) on disk.*

❶ *With several solid backgrounds, this PDF file is 33K (33,251 bytes) on disk.*

❶ *With an image as a background, this PDF file is 41K (40,251 bytes) on disk.*

Backgrounds

I N D E X

Index A

Index S-T

Index U-Z